WESTEND

AF123156

MICHAEL ANDRICK

Empty Success

Philosophy for the World of Work

Translation editing, editing for style, proofreading by
Daniel S. Fisher

WESTEND

More about our authors and books:
www.westendverlag.de
The German National Library lists this publication in the
German National Bibliography; detailed bibliographic
data are available at http://dnb.d-nb.de

The work including all its parts is protected by copyright.
Any exploitation is prohibited without the consent of the
publisher. This applies especially for duplications, translations,
microfilming, and storage and processing in electronic systems.

ISBN: 978-3-86489-497-8
© Westend Verlag GmbH, Waldstr. 12 a, 63263 Neu-Isenburg
Umschlaggestaltung: © Westend Verlag GmbH
Satz: Lumina Datamatics GmbH, Frankfurt am Main

Content

1	**The riddle of our normality**	9
2	**The Craft of Life**	17
	What is our Zeitgeist?	17
	Concepts of Value	19
	Telling our story	24
	Philosophizing is the craft of life	25
	What is morality?	28
	The emergence of our situation	30
3	**Morality and conformity**	35
	Becoming a member and remaining independent	35
	The silent power of reflection	38
	How functionaries die	40
	How people stay alive	47
4	**The order of prestige**	53
	Our self-evident principles and their predecessors	53
	The pressure of centuries	58
	Communication breakdown	61
	The social framework of honor	65
	Respect as a cult of authority	69
	Ascribed Personality	71
	Social Navigation	73
5	**Redemption in success?**	77
	Distractive stress	79
	Standardized identity: Introducing careers	81
	Religion of the functionary	82
	The Myth of success	87
	The Dignity of profit	92
	The pseudo-moral façade	95

6	**How the 'world of work' replaces reality**	**99**
	A world of work?	100
	The path to a world of 'worlds'	103
	Displacement of the real	107
	Rationality and reason	109
	Living in reality	112
7	**Professionalism and the management of 'human capital'**	**115**
	Professionalism as liberating obedience	117
	Leadership is the art of change	124
	Who can lead?	126
	Moral pitfalls of change	129
	The permanent moral crisis of leadership	134
	The Alibi of Relativism	138
8	**Ambition and death**	**145**
	Telling the truth	146
	Approaching ambition	148
	The emptiness of honor	151
	Ambition is pseudo-moral madness	155
	The usual fate	159
	A personal way out	164

The danger of machines transforming people is not particularly great; much greater is the threat that, alongside the machines, changed men will appear in the world: Men like machines, obeying impulses without having the possibility to examine them in their own way.

(Harry Mulisch)

We became – I can't think of another word for it – too much of a herd animal… Indeed, a herd animal, a creature of habit; we were – when the orders came, we clicked our heels together and replied "Yes Sir!"

(NS war criminal Adolf Eichmann;
from trial records cited by Harry Mulisch)

Can you give yourself your own evil and your own good, and let your will be your law?

(Friedrich Nietzsche)

Rebecka - I thank you with all my heart for your immense patience with me and my eccentric projects. And for the book title!

1 The riddle of our normality

Why does so much happen in the world that people individually detest and regret? This question seemed to leap out at me from the pages of books and newspapers when I was a teenager, and has remained with me ever since. When I entered the world of work and became a family father, a certain intuition came to me: Somehow the answer to my question about the mystery of our normality must have something to do with what the world of work does to us. So I resolved to find out exactly what happens to us in the institutions that we pass through, and that often employ us. The result is a book for everyone who goes to work. It began as a lengthy diary entry; it evolved into a philosophy for the world of work.

At the outset, there was astonishment about myself and about us. In the industrialized world of today, our everyday life is based on the disenfranchisement and physical exploitation of people as 'human resources'. It relies for its sustenance on the calculated destruction of the planet's ecosystem. The gimmicks and gadgets of consumption that fill our leisure time are acquired for deceptively low prices; our all-inclusive vacations exploit underpaid service personnel so we can feast at lavish breakfast buffets that we travel to on government-subsidized jet fuel. The bill for our immense 'purchasing power' is paid in the Global South, where the balance is settled for us by the destitute of the southern social hemisphere not in Dollars or Euros, but through the suffering of their families, through hopelessness and despair.

This order of affairs is upheld by preferential, factually colonial trade policies and government subsidies of the rich countries, aided as required by military and financial coercion. While playing along with this rigged game in the daily routine of our working lives, the evening news assures us that "the world economy is growing." So we recline comfortably and rejoice that all is well. Industrial society in its globalized form has all but devoured basic human empathy, sidelining human solidarity to make room for larger and larger transfers accruing to the bank accounts of those that know no hunger, but die of their gluttony instead.

We have created a remarkable culture indeed; the crew of just a single subway car in our cities unites in its daily work the most wildly disparate aims and pursuits, all coexisting as parts of our industrial civilization in morally indifferent comfort and equanimity. In our industrial order, many small actions being executed everyday amount to a global routine operation that each day ignores human suffering and the unfolding ecological catastrophes. Let's take a closer look at our normality. What do we find?

We disseminate misinformation to protect profits, for example in the tobacco, oil or sugar industries; we generally devote a large percentage of our total economic activity to inflated, misleading marketing propaganda, for example, targeting parents and their children with advertisements for unhealthy food which makes their infants chronically (but profitably) ill at an early age; we produce anti-personnel mines that mutilate children at play after the soldiers have left; we devise papers with which we speculate on the declining price of precisely those 'financial products' that we only yesterday sold as an investment to our own bank customers, thereby destroying their savings. Recently, in the United States of America, Great Britain and Turkey (and formerly in Germany), we falsify 'evidence' to justify wars of aggression in which hundreds of thousands of innocent people are killed or expelled from their homes, and exposed to torture and rape, so that access to natural resources can be secured and the domestic military oligarchy can be maintained. We like to drive around in heavy steel cages with leather interiors and combustion engines; we use disposable products for everyday meals, ultimately feeding our plastic to the fish in the seas; we subsidize our agricultural products in such a way that farmers in poorer parts of the world become uncompetitive; and we let those who flee from the misery we help to create for them drown in our bordering seas, while welcoming the survivors with boarder fences studded with razor blades; we make health care a business in some places, thereby letting insufficiently rich people go bankrupt and die when they fall ill, and so on.

The constant "we" in these remarks may be offensive, but let's hold off on that for the moment. Many of the results of our civilization are undeniably ghastly. This might seem obscure to us in the comforts of our daily lives and in the selective and affirmative picture of our world typically conveyed to us by commercial mainstream media. Some phenomena we just discussed can perhaps be ascribe to abnormally cruel individuals, criminal politicians, or the imperial politics of the current great powers. But most of these grievances are brought about by our own work and our own consumer behavior. And we authorize our representatives to perpetuate them - if only out of apathy, disinterest, and ignorance. All of the above mentioned practices are established in our society as the legitimate work of politics and gainful employment, or they represent legal pastimes in which we engage at our leisure and pleasure.

That is why the above facts and realities all correspond to professional titles that have an entirely 'respectable' status in Western societies. These include: public relations consultants, marketing experts or sales strategists, defense (i.e., attack) engineers and armaments managers, financial consultants or 'investment bankers', presidents of the United States, providers of security services, automotive engineers, farmers' association representatives, interior ministers, travel agents, etc. These professions are almost never carried out by criminals, and yet they achieve shameful results with bureaucratic reliability – through co-production between various spheres of professional work.

But how does this happen? How does industrial society achieve our conformism - our practically unreserved complicity in line with almost *any* conceivable purpose, it be what it may? This question has to be posed simply because it is we who exercise the above professions. We run the industrial society that produces these disastrous results while we wallow in the vague and comfortable delusion that we ourselves are not responsible for the misery of the world. But it is obvious that we alone are responsible for this; there is no moral being on earth other than man who can bear responsibility for this state of civilization. So how do we conceal our factual actions from ourselves and from each other? How do we make each other unaware of what we actually know about ourselves and our actions on a daily basis, as if we were living in a state of permanent moral anesthesia? This is the riddle of our normality.

It should be noted here that this normality has not come about recently, it represents the confluence of many historical factors over a long stretch of time. In the more recent stages of this development in the 20th and 21st centuries, wars, brutal oppression of whole populations, and genocide stand out only as islands of particularly intense destruction. The answer to the question of how our present, individual everyday conformism is possible, must therefore also shed new light on this history. It will provide us with a new approach to questions like the following: How were the utterly merciless, cynically calculated campaigns to annihilate innocent peoples possible? How was it possible to impose an economic order throughout the world that is based on the wasteful consumption of raw materials - and that, in a form of ruthless rationality, destroys the environment and produces radical social and economic inequality?

With this brief sketch of our enigmatic normality, we have cast light on a complex of issues requiring explanation. We now have to explore how this state of human affairs came about, which is as comfortable for affluent Westerners as it is absurd on the whole. And we need to understand what this state of affairs implies for our personal lives. An obvious starting point for this clarification would be the adoption of a historical perspective. The historian wants to know, for example, how exactly certain crimes were committed and, in each case, under what specific circumstances. At some point, socially accepted crimes - just like those that are part of our current global normality - will be placed in a broader context and in this way made more or less comprehensible.

This book, on the other hand, has the intention of adopting a philosophical approach to the mystery and solving it. We will address historical events here and there, but our guiding question is not how exactly something happened historically. The philosophical question in which we are interested is whether the typical patterns of events reveal a logic of their own. We are looking for the principle of our enigmatic normality, its driving motives, patterns of thought and behavior - and their origin. On the basis of which known forces and their interaction can we expect the dramatic grievances of our normality? How can the inhumane aspects of industrial society function just as systematically and smoothly as, for instance, the payment of social benefits in western social democracies? And if that is the case, how are we all somehow involved in this system? How can we protect ourselves from its unscrupulousness? And above all, how can we change it?

For me, philosophical research always begins with a few more or less linked initial insights and intuitions, coupled with a penetrating curiosity or indignation - in any case, there is a kind of frenzy for clarification that is driving me. The concrete combination of assumptions, suspicions and intentions that motivate this book, results from the peculiar mix of 'ingredient experiences' of my own life so far. I would like to mention these briefly because they shed some light on the style and also the dominant interests pursued in this work.

As a manager, I lead a rather typical professional life, but with an atypical academic background in philosophy and history. That is why I am familiar with the hopelessly boring and pointless alignment meetings among colleagues and with the no less oppressive boredom of high-brow, pseudo-intellectual waffling on Plato and Hegel in stuffy seminar rooms. However, I also know the fun of good cooperation on successful business projects and the fascination of an academic discussion in which the students actually come to understand and appreciate something of value and human importance.

My everyday life is characterized by rational work with mostly clear objectives, in the company that employs me. But my formal training is in the exercise of reason, independent of particular, preconceived ends (philosophy). Correspondingly, I have been able to try my hand at the intellectual treatment of broad questions as well as at the pragmatic resolution of economic problems. In this way, I have learned from my own experience about the structures and forces at play in our institutions. My expertise in the conceptual gymnastics of philosophy that fill my late evenings to this day shapes my writing as much as my business experience as a manager does. It is on this basis that I hope to offer some fresh perspectives on our world of work - without resorting either to intellectual jargon, or to the platitudes of business literature.

To get started, we will first want to take a step back from these introductory remarks, carefully preparing ourselves for a series of reflections that should, taken together, yield a sharpened understanding of our present society and situation. It is not that we 'drop' the thread of the initial diagnosis now, only to 'pick it back up' a few chapters later. On the contrary, we will now look at the fibers from which this thread is spun and whose fabric has become our reality.

The conceptual means by which we can recognize the pattern of this fabric more clearly, and ultimately decide if we like it, will be acquired step by step. Various aspects of the initial consideration of the riddle of our normality continually play a role; but it is precisely at the beginning of this intellectual journey that we also need to introduce some basic philosophical considerations. With these to build on, we can then work out, step by step, the logic of our fateful normality. One need not be an experienced philosopher to embark on this journey with me, but one must be determined to philosophize.

Chapters 2 and 3 provide a brief introduction to the practical significance of philosophy for social beings like us. It is especially close to my heart to show that philosophizing is not an expert activity detached from the lives of 'ordinary people,' but rather a natural activity for every human being. The fourth chapter explains how a specific logic of prestige and status emerged historically that has since come to determine everyday life in our work-centered societies and to structure our behavior.

The following four chapters then deal with different aspects of our lives in different 'work-worlds', or spheres professional routine. We will outline and attempt to fathom, first, the peculiar form of salvation that the rational pursuit of success seems to bring us ("Redemption in success?"). Next, we consider the distance from reality we may drift into while doing our daily work ("How the world of work replaces reality"). The following chapter deals with the interplay between professionalism and leadership that produces a mutilated form of human interaction in our institutions ("Distorted Humanity"). Finally, we will bring into sharp focus the ambition that drives our careers and that, upon closer analysis, actually turns out to be a specific kind of madness ("Ambition and Death").

This step-by-step construction of our reflection is not merely useful for solving the riddle of our normality. It also corresponds to the philosophical task presented to each of us as individuals. Whether or not we will find contentment and make peace with our ambitions and individual fate depends very much on how we imagine the circumstances confronting us. This is, in fact, a tall order because the present in which a person finds himself is always more complicated than he can possibly understand.

Past suffering and euphoria, the flimsy patchwork of our memories, our immersion in the – digital or paper - 'filter bubbles' of like-minded people, and, finally, the half-digested, half-forgotten chunks of knowledge from our school days - all of this contributes to make us the particular person that we are. But it certainly does not lead us to an objective point of view, that is, to a viewpoint based in consideration and judgement that is fair to things and people. Moreover, it is the present and its greater and smaller rulers who have the power to distribute jobs and the amenities of life. We therefore have a strong incentive to accept the present conditions of society as "the solution" or "the way things have to be" - we do not primarily and naturally want to ask questions, criticize or enhance our understanding. We want admission to the club, and to participate and share in the rewards (or spoils) there.

It is therefore unrealistic to think that we simply understand our own present situation and assess it realistically. Nevertheless, we must understand ourselves in the context of the social moment we are in the light of the basic forces at play there. To set out on a journey, the first thing one needs to know is where one actually is. In order to imagine our surroundings correctly, it is necessary to reach into the past and to engage in a targeted exercise of reflection. One must consciously and deliberately examine the images and prejudices he has grown accustomed to in order to avoid being misled. In the course of the book's progression, we will therefore repeatedly take up and examine familiar terms and ways of thinking, and while proceeding to use them, we will modify their meaning to enable fresh insights. This requires some work, but enlightenment entails work - just as life itself consists of working on oneself in the light of experience.

2 The Craft of Life

What is our Zeitgeist?

Let us begin our approach to philosophy by thinking about language, the instrument of philosophy and the medium in which it has to take place. Our language is where our thoughts and feelings live, very much as one dwells in an apartment. The rooms, corridors and walls of this home are familiar to us. But we did not design and build them ourselves, we have simply grown up within them. The floor plan of our language allows some insights and views to come to us naturally, effortlessly. Other realizations, however, are obstructed as if by walls because our language does not offer us concepts and images with which we could render them insights.

Considered in its entirety, our language contains a certain image of reality. For example, an exploration of our use of big words like 'freedom' or 'justice' shows us what we actually mean by these terms. By the same token, analyzing 'smaller,' more specific linguistic habits can reveal our habitual view of the world with its many inconspicuous absurdities. For example, most working people in Germany call themselves *Arbeitnehmer* (employee; literally: "receiver or taker of work"). On the other side of the equation, we call the person or institution that employs us *Arbeitgeber* (employer, literally: "provider or giver of work"). But it is actually exactly the other way round, as Friedrich Engels once remarked: *We give* our labor to an institution in return for money, *the institution* receives, or takes, our work. In fact, working people are "givers of work" (*Arbeitgeber*), while companies, administrations and many other institutions are the actual "receivers or takers of work" (*Arbeitnehmer*). The language Germans are accustomed to obstructs them from gaining insight into this.

Each sentence we form is based on the whole reality that our language, viewed as an entirety, represents; each sentence leads us to a fixed point within the boundaries of this worldview. How we have learned to choose our words reveals the mental dwelling in which our thinking, feeling and doing has established itself. The ground plan of our language therefore shows the Zeitgeist of our present. The Zeitgeist tells us who we are, how we fit in among other people and into the world, and what we may hope for, fear, and realistically expect. The Zeitgeist rules the world through our thinking, speaking and doing. For example, the Zeitgeist embodied in the German language would have us believe that we are (grateful?) *Arbeitnehmer* ("receivers or takers of work") and that others are our (generous?) *Arbeitgeber* ("providers or givers of work"). "Putting one word in the place of another means changing the view of the social world and thereby contributing to its transformation" (Pierre Bourdieu).

To reflect means to question the spirit of the times. To pose a question actually means to rehearse the rebellion against our sentences: against the claim of their supposed truths to our faith and our loyalty. To ask questions is to pause in speaking and thinking; questioning means interrupting the normal course of events and flow of things at the handrail provided courtesy of our Zeitgeist, in favor of reflection. To ask many questions means rehearsing the rebellion against the whole worldview of our Zeitgeist. Only with this fundamental reflection do we begin to exist as persons and not just as a walking and talking result of our life circumstances. Our reflection is essentially self-assertion; struggle against the customs and habits of mind and of action that hold us firmly in their grip. In other words: Only questioning and reflecting turn this sentient ego, in which all manner of perceptions arise, stir and disappear again, into a self - into myself. "Personality (...) is the simple, almost automatic result of thoughtfulness" (Hannah Arendt).

In order to live life as *ourselves* - i.e., by our own lights and precepts and not simply as incarnated expressions of what we have been accustomed to - we must escape the regime of the Zeitgeist. In many instances, people manage this without notable effort or endless brooding, simply by virtue of a propitious combination of experiences and encounters over the course of their lives: Their family lets them feel that they are wanted and loved, allowing them to develop a secure sense about who they want to be as adults; they find their way with a sense of agency and calm. Over time, they discover what it is that is worthy of their best efforts; what others say and want is interesting for them, but not decisive. Many, however, are not this lucky - something disturbs their circles or is missing from them that could grant them this calm self-determination. A guiding feeling for the meaning and direction of their lives does not arise in them, instead, a stubborn and unsettling question surfaces: How did I come to be this way? And what is it about myself that I just cannot seem to be satisfied?

To address this question, to come to ourselves, we need an explanation of our Zeitgeist - a philosophy of our present that makes comprehensible for us how we have learned to think, speak and live as we do now. Only on this basis can we ourselves then ask, reflect and act – for one thing, in order to forge our own path in life within the constraints of our society; but also, and equally important, to contribute alongside others to shaping the politics of our society. Without having a philosophy of our present age at our disposal, it is really just our Zeitgeist speaking through us. We live then as puppets of the past, and perhaps, if we are ambitious, as the puppeteers of the present, but without thereby coming to ourselves. Let us therefore begin our philosophical journey where it will end: let us start with ourselves, and hope that we will find greater clarity and sense of purpose than we can muster at the outset.

Concepts of Value

"Coming to oneself" - that sounds as if the self is already there, like a particularly precious object in the household of our soul. If that were true, one would only have to see through certain distractions and properly focus on it. But that is not the case. One's self is not already there, and it is therefore wrong to think that one could simply concentrate a little more on it to find and stay the right course for one's life. We all say 'I,' but no 'I' is simply and directly, *unproblematically and immediately* a self.

Only the 'I' that tells of itself makes the self; my self is the *story* of who I am. Only in this sense is it 'already there': I can draw myself again and again as a silhouette from memory, each time a little different. This narrative means everything. It shows my idea of what is worth my effort, on which path my life *as I conceive of it* may succeed and how it could escape my grasp. My story is alive only in the silent conversation of reflection and in trustful exchange with others; my reflective narrative is an expression of my concepts of value and has no yardstick, no standard except for these to be measured by. A person's moral concepts are crucial to his life because they guide his aspirations, ground his fears, and determine his ambitions.

I imagine the things we value in life to be *absent* from view for us, or at least perceived only vaguely - that's why I speak of *concepts of value* (*Wertvorstellungen*), and not straightforwardly of *values*. This particular choice of words indicates that I do not directly and reliably recognize the value of certain things, certain behaviors and attitudes. I merely *imagine* or *believe* that they have a value. The difficulty with moral concepts is not only my personal problem; the fact that I am used to talking and thinking in this way rather expresses a certain *knowledge* that is characteristic for our culture.

If I take only myself into consideration, I think I know which things I value and why. But from another person's point of view, this, *my* conviction can only be considered soberly as a set of specific *value concepts*. For it actually turns out differently, what different people think that they have recognized as valuable. So we live with the difficulty that our subjective insights into what is valuable are constantly challenged by other people's value judgements. These others judge in the same way as we do, based on their own special life experience. We can recognize these differences as long as we are at home in the same mental dwelling place, i.e., in the same language as the others. However, real, substantial differences remain.

From this reality we learn to talk about our *concepts of value* and to put them into perspective before any possible discussion. We talk about our values, i.e., what is important to us in life, while at the same time questioning them. We do not treat any other significant concept with which we navigate our world in such a manner; we do not, for example, speak with the same fluency of our 'concept of freedom' or our 'concept of justice' - we simply speak of freedom and justice. But we speak of concepts of value.

This hesitant, problematizing attitude with regard to our personal values is understandable and perfectly justified. Unlike statements, for example, about the world of material things we share - tables, chairs and ashtrays - we do not believe that our society has a natural consensus of opinion on questions of value. That is why we do not readily trust ourselves to have convincing answers to questions of value, nor in our society do we learn to cultivate a desire for such knowledge in the first place. This, however, stands in tension with the earlier statement that our life as a person crucially depends on the concepts of value we hold.

How many times have we heard someone ask: "What is the right thing to do in this situation? What should I do?" No matter how many times we may have heard and discussed such questions, these experiences certainly fade in the face of the never-ending negotiations around the question "What do I (really) want?" that we tend to go through with ourselves and others. If we report on the course of our individual lives with their respective twists and turns, we often talk about what we liked at what time - what was pleasant for us, what began or ceased to bring us pleasure. This is often a point of departure for explaining what we ended up doing or leaving undone.

I am referring here to a mentality, a habitual state of mind that can be observed in us - not to a 'mistake' that we make. For this intellectual attitude is not absurd. As regards our concepts of value, we "play it by ear." In the course of our lives, only concrete experiences show us the unique richness that a certain attitude, a certain relationship to others, or a certain good brings to our life. One has experience after it would have been needed. For example, it cannot be fully understood and appreciated in advance that having children of one's own changes *everything* - and that therefore the question whether life is 'better' with or without children is nonsensical.

Though understandable, the mindset that tells the story of one's own life as the story of changing likes and dislikes, is completely caught up in the given Zeitgeist: If we merely explain what we like, we are in fact only explaining what concepts of value we have been taught - or else we are simply revealing what we have unconsciously adopted. We recite, so to speak, the Zeitgeist (just as we would recite a memorized poem) and allow it to lead us in this or that direction, in the course of our changing involvements, entanglements, and experiences. In this state of mind, the crucial question of which destination is worthwhile aiming for – the question of what is actually of value to us - is not yet posed. In this way, we do not learn the craft to live as a self, as *ourselves.*

In each epoch this craft of life can be different; perhaps in some periods of our European history it was not even necessary as such because a strong and tightly interwoven community gave us credible answers to questions of value before we had to ask them. In any case, however, we must understand what this craft of life is *today and for us*. To succeed in this, we must above all reflect on our peculiar *alienation* from the considerations of value that we have just remarked upon. This phenomenon has to do with how the individual can experience the value of things for himself.

A close-knit tribal or feudal society directly conveys the practical meaning of certain demands on the individual. The justification of these demands is obvious and subsequently creates the idea that something is of value. Respect and obedience to father and mother, for example, are not controversial when it is *only they* who can feed us and when the only religion we have ever known commands such obedience. Reliability in the observance of one's own duties rewards the member of such a society with the acceptance of those with whom he will be associated for a long time, if not for his whole life.

In European modernity, by contrast, experiences conveying to us a sense of the value of practically anything are more complicated than that. These experiences are no longer as small-scale, immediate and directly convincing as they were in pre-modern times. Above all, value-related experiences here and now are not so regularly linked to concrete people who are of lasting importance for our well-being. The people who remain with us today for part of our journey - schoolmates, army comrades, neighbors - are like passengers in a tram who unexpectedly get on and off again, who may be close to us in the meantime, but who will not usually form part of our permanent circle of friends and associates. Even between parents and their children, the rule of law has introduced regulations to guarantee certain entitlements regardless of the quality of personal relationships.

Work in our societies is divided into areas of expertise that are often narrowly defined; all concrete activities and concerns become abstract through their evaluation and negotiation in financial terms; even the most modest modern life has an enormous spatial radius of action. This is often accompanied, whether admittedly or not, by a certain *friendlessness* in the course of the lives we lead. We seem to no longer have a natural, intimate home sphere, unless we know how to create it for ourselves. In addition, there is a variety of diverse and yet frequently reasonable ways of looking at this state of affairs. All these are hallmarks of a life situation in which we usually speak to one other about *concepts of value* and not simply and directly about *values*.

When we express ourselves in this way, we are not claiming that there are no *real* - as opposed to just imagined, or invented – values, and therefore no true morals. For the purposes of the philosophy we are here beginning to unfold, we do not have to answer this question, which is characteristic for skeptical, doubt-ridden epochs that find themselves confronted with an unmanageable pace of change and chaos of experience. Our language of *value concepts* reveals an arrangement that we have developed in the face of disagreement about ultimate truths in order to preserve the peace. We need only to build on this insight to advance in our philosophy for the world of work – and we can leave an examination of the question which moral principles we have best reason to adopt for another book.

Telling our story

In the intellectual and moral climate of our society, only conscious reflection allows us to come to a personal best guess about what we should deem to be essential for our life. This is exactly what it means for the individual to live in the modern age: Most of us do not inherit a solid knowledge of what is valuable, the observance of which we could then practice in community with others. The communities that believe they have such knowledge, that teach and cultivate it, have been on the retreat for centuries. Therefore, we have to create our own knowledge of what is valuable ; we have to *experience* it for ourselves, much as we would explore a city we have not yet visited.

To live like this requires a special craft of self-management. We need a routine to develop our own value concepts, to validate them through experience and to give birth to ourselves as a personality in this protracted, unsteady process. Modern man is not simply there, he is *himself*. To be a self, the self that corresponds to the man we refer to when we say 'I,' requires the ability to narrate oneself. In other words: I become myself by telling my story. The practical significance of philosophy for every human being is closely related to this fact, as we will soon see.

The story of who I am - as myself, that is - can never again be told in exactly the same way as I would tell it today. That is what it means to be alive and not dead: that I am both being formed and forming myself; that I am well known to myself and yet constantly and gradually becoming somebody slightly different as I tell my story. I react to my experience in a silent conversation with myself by *reflecting on* my encounters with things, forces and people. I imagine this as a practice of literally thinking around and through these objects of my attention, examining their connections and distances, their likenesses and differences. In doing so, what is new and strange in my experience is confronted with my story, and may in various ways become interwoven with it.

The new and the strange in my experience thus becomes my own; either in the negative sense that I choose to defend myself against it, or in the constructive sense that I include some of it into my self-narrative. This constant 'incorporating' of my experience into my story means that I influence myself *because I* (and *while I*) am encountering new influences. My present is the place where my self-narration sets me down, thus, a stopover the view from which narrows my options and orients my further journey, but which never completely determines it. The Latin proverb *mutatis mutamur* is incomplete; not "As those who have been changed, we change" - but "As those who have been changed, we change ourselves." And only then do we change other things as well as others we meet.

My life stands at any given time under a thousand conditions; but I also place *my* conditions on myself and others. This is the work of life: the endurance of things and of the others and the work of creating and maintaining myself with them and against them. All this happens in the knowledge of my certain death and therefore with the dramatic aspect of a unique opportunity. The memory built in the process is our life experience; the mental and emotional horizon that we open up for ourselves in the process is our life wisdom. But our capacity for human solidarity is not determined by our life experience and wisdom. Showing solidarity means to observe and feel with others, guided by the intention to share in their burden, acknowledging the commonalities of our fates, not just verbally, but through action. Humanity is always personal, concrete and momentary; it is manifested in those instances in which we truly pay attention to the concerns of others and try as their fellows to partake in their struggles.

Philosophizing is the craft of life

I understand philosophy as the attempt to turn the work of life into a craft through reflection. (The expression "The craft of life" was coined by Cesare Pavese, but he does not use it to refer to philosophy).

Whoever now thinks of carpenters and shoemakers and their crafts has already grasped the meaning of this peculiar expression. For only if the thinking of philosophy can be practically translated into our lives, i.e., *exercised,* is it ultimately worth the effort. Philosophizing means consciously working to become the person we want to be for ourselves and others.

Part of this craft entails specifically seeking out experiences that we hope will help us make progress along this path. If I want to be a credible leader who works effectively and harmoniously with different kinds of people, I will want to expose myself to the most difficult, perhaps overburdening leadership tasks. These activities will provide me with experiences and insights that will make me more prudent and wise for my own specific path in life. In this way, I will gain the wisdom that *my* life requires. This is how I learn the craft of my life.

The thoughtful and practical effort to achieve a life in tune with my concepts of value is philosophy; a constant effort to lead my life *myself.* An unreflected life is simply an existence in time - it does not succeed or fail because it makes no demands on the progress of things. Industrial society obscures this fact and induces us to miss life.

A life that follows my rule and my intention, on the other hand, is a committed life that will achieve or miss its fulfillment and satisfaction. This is what Plato means when he lets Socrates say that a life lived in unreflected routine is not worth living. The question that confronts us is this: How must I think and act in order, when the one and only opportunity arises, to live in the right way?

Have I found the craft of my life, my philosophy? And if so, have I practically mastered it or am I just prattling? The theoretical antics of academic philosophy, its conceptual contortions that seem ridiculous to the everyday mind of the 'uninitiated' and its elaborate reassurances about apparently very simple things - all this does not represent the ends of philosophy, but a means of philosophy, the essential purpose of which is to help us live. Theory is not the final aim of philosophy, as it is not the final aim of life. Rather, it is the exploration of the path to our aims; at the end of *my* path to *my* aim.

To openly dedicate oneself to the craft of one's life, one's philosophy, has its costs. Philosophizing manifests itself in a general reluctance to get involved and go along with others, which can appear as a lack of sociability and sympathy. Those who question themselves must ultimately also answer to themselves, and are therefore often found alone and often need to be. And the self-questioning of a philosopher is perceived by others - especially, but not only, when he speaks. Thoughtfulness is also conveyed through gestures, glances, conscious pausing and the visible degrees of interest and distraction.

Thoughtfulness in a person can also be a real and present threat – for those people who want to be assured of the correctness of their views and do not wish to be unsettled. The greatest intuitive opponents of philosophy are people who suffer from their lives, but who have made the greatest effort to shape them just as they are. People who are particularly successful in the conventional sense often nip any thoughtfulness in the bud, in their leisure activities and in conversation, to ensure that (to use Nietzsche's apt expression) the bow of their previous life will not break.

These last remarks may conjure up the typical image of the philosopher as an eccentric, unworldly loner who arrogantly judges others - a popular cliché that is comfortable for everyone involved. For it relieves the philosopher of his silent fear, indeed his trauma, of being connected to the 'real world' or 'real life' in a meaningful way and perhaps of not being able to strike that connection; it also relieves his fellow men of taking philosophizing seriously, since its representatives are obviously quixotic crackpots.

The fantasy of the unworldly philosopher is useful and effective to escape from thinking about oneself. But this presumption is ultimately misleading. Philosophizing is not an exceptional and difficult state of mind that rarely occurs, nor is it a stage of development to be passed through. Philosophizing is the intellectual and practical activity by which mere existence in the ups and downs of experience becomes the *life* of a particular individual. Our philosophizing is therefore inseparably bound up in our morality, which cannot at all be consciously brought to bear in our lives without philosophical reflection.

What is morality?

At this point, things seem to become more difficult because morality is often discussed as a matter at once both vague and infinitely complicated. When talking about 'morality,' one might imagine a small number of brooding individuals wrapped in cigarette smoke making profound statements with a penetrating gaze – statements that it would seem irreverent to understand at first hearing. Or one thinks of self-important moral sermons, the likes of which politicians or clergymen are known to give on Sundays and in places where all can see them. But if we ignore this tradition of mystification and pathetic coloring of the matter, it becomes clear and simple.

To be a moral being means to be able to have a silent conversation with oneself. Whoever talks to himself asks himself questions and replies to himself, makes remarks, builds bridges from one point of view to another, admits old mistakes and gains new insights. In short, whoever talks to himself retains a reservation about what is momentarily going through his head and limbs. For the ideas and assumptions that occupy my mind and drive my actions could at any one moment be nonsense or unfair, and further conversation with myself and thoughtful exchange with others could well teach me that. Whoever talks to himself wants to know what he *really* has reason to believe and do. Andrej Platonov must have had this in mind when saying that "talking to oneself is an art, talking to other people is distraction."

In talking to ourselves, we not only criticize our own ideas and conceptions; our inner dialogue also marks a reservation against our usual actions and the expectable behavior in our surroundings. What we are just 'now' thinking is questioned by and for ourselves, and therefore we do not simply do what our current thinking suggests to us, nor do we accept this from others, either. We hesitate and take another look. To be moral means to speak to oneself and thus to reserve for oneself the last word, which we as humans actually have over our circumstances. Moral reflection becomes moral action if we then also actually speak this last word and bear the consequences.

Our moral capacity lies in reflection and action. In reflection we maintain a reservation about what we find; in action we object to what is happening around us and stand up for what we think is better. Our morality is the veto that we reserve for ourselves against our own momentary will, against the actions of others, but especially against the seductive pull to join in the chorus of the actual or perceived majority. The technical term in philosophy for this active, permanently concerned form of self-determination is *autonomy*: an autonomous, i.e., a 'self-governing' being is one that can rethink and alter its own standards of evaluation and patterns of behavior.

Conceived in this way, philosophizing is the actual, characteristic activity of a moral being. For by determining the goals of our lives and the craft of their pursuit, we bring values into the world. This is our reservation against the established course of things, our first truly personal word and at the same time the last word we will insist on where it is in dispute. Herein lies the hope of being able to move beyond the distress of our current life and the cruel ills of our inherited world to something better. Here, in our autonomy, lies our solitary dignity.

It would therefore be a complete misunderstanding to regard the reflection on questions of principle, the good life and a just society as the business of some kind of specialized elite. Pub conversations and endless phone calls between siblings and friends revolve around the experiences that give rise to the questions about the right crafting of one's own life. Even if the questions of philosophy are not raised explicitly, they are nevertheless negotiated on these occasions. Being occupied with philosophical questions is something common to everyone, because we are all subject to the same limitations and are bound for the same mortal end. But it does not occur to everyone to call this 'philosophizing.' Nor is it important to name it as such - except perhaps for those who, as 'official' philosophers, are part of a profession and want to be assured of its significance. Fortunately, Franco Berardi is right: "People often act without reading the relevant books."

The emergence of our situation

In summary, we have good reason to understand life as work on ourselves in the light of experience - and philosophy as the search for the right path of this self-design, as the search for the craft of our life. Historically, however, life has also been experienced and imagined in a different way, less as work on oneself and more as assuming our pre-ordained place among others. José Ortega y Gasset speaks of the fact that up to the turn of the modern age, human existence had consisted "in an adaptation to the universe," of which the individual understood himself to be a part. Pre-modern man began his life "with a feeling of confidence in the world" (my translations).

But the great narratives of God, world and man, which granted us this comfort of a permanent, 'official' position in the world order, are no longer convincing; historically, they have proven themselves to be increasingly powerless to bring effective order to human society. God's order is no longer a credible ideological basis for human association. And even if we happen to be believers of this or that creed and religion, we do not try to justify our claims on others with our orthodoxy.

There is no teaching about life that will calm our deepest concerns once and for all and grant us peace of mind; and it may be an idealization to believe that such a moral tale was once available and wholly believable to its followers. Our parents and teachers today cannot simply indicate to us who we are and what the destined place for us in society is. They simply teach and show us that many things are possible for us. We are not actually introduced into our lives, as one might be shown around the house one is to inhabit, but are instead set out in the open with the mandate to be on our way.

How did we get into this situation? Why do we as individuals need to explore, educate and guide ourselves? Why can't we learn the craft of life by quietly watching others who protect and instruct us? The cultural history that has brought us to this point can be told from different perspectives. But the essential development is simple, and it is worthwhile to try and bring it to clarity: The functions of people for one other, which gave them certain powers over one other, became a matter of dispute in late medieval Europe.

This gave rise to extensive and devastating wars during the Reformation and Counter-Reformation periods. A new epoch, the 'modern age' (*Neuzeit*) had to be invented because the old, theologically-based order was no longer able to establish credible and effective authority, and therefore could not achieve a stable peace. In the Peace Treaty of Münster and Osnabrück, which ended the Thirty Years' War in 1648, it was therefore agreed that questions of religious truth would not be the subject of negotiations. The warring parties knew that they would not be able to find common ground if each party invoked 'the truth.'

The historian of ideas Hans Blumenberg says of the transition to the modern age (*Neuzeit*): "The Middle Ages came to an end when, within its theological system, creation could no longer credibly be maintained as 'providence' for man, thus imposing on him the burden of his own self-assertion." This development began with the emergence of the *nominalist* philosophy of the late Middle Ages - a theoretical approach in which language is seen as purely human-conventional: Our concepts are simply names (*nomina*), i.e., appellations of things. This expresses the then revolutionary idea that names chosen by man create the conceptual order of our thought and language - and not God's act of creation at the beginning of the world.

According to this line of historical interpretation, the loss of existential stability suffered in late medieval times comes to light in the fact that language as a bridge between thought and the world was no longer naively trusted. Our concepts for that which appears in consciousness obey no natural law, but only human arbitrariness; all semblance of authority and duration in our thought and language is thus owed solely to the weight of tradition, the simple repetition of certain linguistic conventions by many over many generations. *We* are now the ones establishing the order we see in the world.

Alasdair MacIntyre describes from a different vantage point this same loss of stability as the slow decline of the concept of virtue. Virtues are historically tested and proven ways to win for oneself humanly significant goods: honesty, for example, is a virtue because it establishes trust in and brings reliability to our relationships. Thus, the practice of honesty can bring us stability, peace and serenity. According to MacIntyre's narrative, virtues could be learned in community through imitation and exchange until the end of the Middle Ages; a broad consensus on the meaning and requirements of individual virtues could effectively regulate our comportment in society. For in a community that is crowded in a narrowly restricted space and largely united in faith, a certain practice of life is shared by virtually all its members. This practice brings forth standards of value and stabilizes them over generations.

From today's point of view, this vision appears idyllic, a state of all-pervading moral harmony (at least if one experiences the present as socially fragmented, complex, and perhaps even uncanny). For according to this view, a reliable practical orientation is slowly evolving in every member of the community. In such a society, value concepts and demands on each individual continue, of course, to change, but never in an erratic or threatening way. This state of harmony was definitely lost with the advent of denominational divisions in Christianity.

It was replaced, MacIntyre feels, by the unfortunate and ill-fated project of justifying morality by means of philosophical argumentation - instead of bringing it to bear directly through living examples and discussions in clearly bounded, rather small-scaled communities. The modern need for intellectual justification of our morality and traditions demonstrates that for us 'modernists' there is no common reality of life that is simply understood as natural and accepted unequivocally as fact.

Blumenberg and MacIntyre reflect on the same process in different ways: human will assumes the power and responsibility to determine by its own lights the value of all things. Man becomes the measure of all things, sovereign of the world and of all life in it. The major features and traditions of the world in which we grew up and live today all refer back to this initial defining moment. "Sin can no longer be defined as disobedience to the law of another, but on the contrary as a refusal to play my role as the legislator of the world" (Hannah Arendt on Kant's philosophy).

The Enlightenment further shaped this fundamental reference to human will into the idea of a general dominion of reason, and attempted to make reason prevail in all areas of human interest; the scientific-industrial revolution, in conjunction with the modern state, then divided our world into rational institutions, each organized for a specific purpose. But the intellectual, moral, and political center of this whole development was and is the self-sufficient will of man left to its own devices.

In this way, we have gone from being children of God and members of his flock on earth to being the narrators of our social history and, individually, of ourselves. In this way, philosophy, once understood as the steward of eternal truths, has been transformed into a quest of our individual reflection for the craft of our lives. Within these coordinates, we now go in search of the configuration and the peculiar inner coherence of our present age. It will prove to be an age of career and a special form of moral numbness, which I associate with the concept of ambition. The next step in this journey is to investigate the fundamental tension between morality and social conformity.

3 Morality and conformity

Becoming a member and remaining independent

To live together in a mass society, its members must comport themselves with predictability. Because we never know who we are dealing with, except in our families and our circle of friends. The others must be able to anticipate my motives and behavior, depending on the situation at hand. Being *socially acceptable* means maintaining a certain standard and therefore being reliable and safe for others to deal with. This is something that we find self-evident in our lives and that is worth considering separately in some depth for once: for it follows from the reflections in the previous chapter that we as modern people are not simply and without any doing of our own – *in society* at all times. To begin, we are merely in a group of people.

To exist *socially*, that is, in such a way that we are predictable for one other, is something one must now *learn*; it does not come to us naturally or through an unequivocal tradition. The group into which we are born and in which we grow up is only one among many in our society. Each group's respective concepts of value and habits can differ greatly from those of other circles of people. It is therefore a distinct task for us to learn to live together with members of all different kinds of groups and to play roles acceptable to them. We need 'social competence,' the learned ability to play our part in mass society.

On the interpersonal level, this reflects exactly what we thought through in the second chapter. The individual must give himself a self, i.e., by reflecting on his experience and by constantly telling and retelling his own story, give birth to himself as a personality. Similarly, we establish ourselves socially by learning the rules of our society and by constantly practicing them as its members. Our fellow members of society can only undertake or continue with us the different projects of community life, as long as we are in conformance with the shared societal norms and thus found to be socially acceptable.

For the society we form with others is, as Norbert Elias writes, the "invisible order from which and into which the individuals set their purposes." If we disregard the rules of our society and thereby affect people who do not belong to our circle of confidants, we fundamentally irritate them. They can no longer be sure of our cooperation to further *their* own aims. The degree of our conformity demonstrates to the others to what extent we are willing to support the current social system and the power relations embodied in it. Our conformity documents for them that we are participating, accepting of a reality we share with them – *and* that we can therefore also be trusted to guarantee *their* ability to act in their own interests when relevant occasions for them to do so arise.

Any society continues to exist only by instilling in its members precisely the behavior, the patterns of thought and emotion, that correspond to the specific power relations of that given society. Only in this way, can any society, viewed as a coherent system, be assured of survival. The people of any given society must become its *members*. To take issue with this and to complain of perfidious manipulation of 'natural man' into a state of moral corruption is to misunderstand the nature of society.

However, a real threat to our morality emanates from the inescapable pressure of every society to conform. We are absolutely dependent for our survival on our belonging to a community. How am I supposed to posit and to maintain a basic reserva-tion for my own moral reflection, a veto against doing what seems to be required of me, when membership can only be se-cured at the price of conformity? How can I be morally independent if at the same time I cannot help but to conform in general to the conditions and authorities in my society?

This is a critical problem of social existence that concerns us all, so let's consider how we could resolve it. Couldn't we just give up on critical thought, on our obstinate insistence to want to know and judge for ourselves? In short, couldn't we simply surrender our morality? In an enlightened society, what should hold us back from this? It would nicely solve the problem of the opposition between morality and social conformity.

This was the argument, for example, offered by historical materialism, the "scientific worldview" of Marxism-Leninism (which should not be confused with Marx' philosophy): Classless society takes shape of its own accord in the course of human history, with scientific certainty, and conforming to this nascent society is identical with being a morally good person. Ethical theories such as utilitarianism, which focuses on the concept of utility, also allow for moral self-abdication and offer a logic of calculation with supposedly known quantities (such as economic utility), as a substitute model for individual moral orientation in life.

Since we are still waiting for the arrival of the classless society just as some are waiting for the return of the Son of God, the Marxist-Leninist solution does not quite convince me. History will appear but to a small minority as the stepwise progression toward classless society, or as God's moral chamber play leading up to Judgement Day. Moreover, a utilitarian becomes embarrassed when you ask him which understanding of 'utility' is the most *useful*.

This question may well seem preposterous, but it is not intended as a joke. To ask it is to pull away the utilitarian's fig leaf: One notices that the notion of utility, which is supposed to solve our moral problems of orientation, is itself vague and open to being interpreted in many ways. So we still have to rely on our moral judgement - if only to decide that we should evaluate and direct our actions according to one and not the other of the many conceivable definitions of "utility". We must remain moral persons *and* gain a foothold in our society.

The silent power of reflection

As long as there are moral persons, and *only as long as they exist*, there is a possibility that the normal course of affairs, the customary behavior, the accepted standard of thinking will be disrupted. Established thought and behavior is under scrutiny and does not simply rule continuously and absolutely according to the prevailing theory and practice, whatever that may be.

Moral persons are the only agents capable of changing the products and machinations of human culture - or who can at least help us escape them. What purpose is served by the whole business of disputing, delaying, complicating and possibly preventing action, that moral persons are engaged in? Well, a moral person has but one essential role: to comprehend the functioning of human beings in given structures and ways of thinking and, where necessary, to change or sabotage such routines.

Thus, the moral person remains whole, i.e., he thereby asserts his integrity: The world, other people and the conditions they create do not dictate what we think and what we do. They are subject to the criticism of our reflection; as moral persons we are the 'measure' of what we do and think. We are not merely the administrators of what others have introduced before us and alongside us. Rather, we are called upon to evaluate, judge, and reform tradition, as we see fit. Integral moral persons are the only guarantee that things with us and our world can be different than they are. They alone uphold human dignity in the face of the perils to which our civilization exposes it. Even if I cannot fulfill it, moral integrity is the right ideal of a free human being who accepts his responsibility.

But how can moral persons of integrity change themselves and the world? Moral persons conduct their lives with their backs turned to the prestige and power of the social structure and its representatives. They do *not* strive for rank and name, they do *not* preoccupy themselves with elaborately planned, wasteful consumption in order to create this or that impression with others or themselves. Nor do they want to be liked in the first place. Instead, they pay close attention to their own ideas of what is valuable in their own lives and for their society. Where everyone looks outward, they look inward; they care about their own integrity.

Perhaps surprisingly, this is the reason why moral persons hold the true and real power in society. They can act in defiance of their society's norms because they know alternatives based on their concepts of value and the work of their reflection. Moral persons can therefore change society; conformists can only oil its wheels and run its various types of machines. This is the astonishing paradox of morality: the moral person gains power over the actual conditions only by *turning away* from them and *turning to* himself. The power of the moral person derives from his refusal to exploit the established patterns of thought and behavior to his advantage. Therefore, the promise of what the powers that be have to offer for his conformity does not have the same disciplining power over him that it has over the majority.

The power of our social and political concepts of value to first envision and then create a different future is based on the fact that moral persons consciously accept their *immediate powerlessness* in society and are thereby able to build up a truly independent will to act. This movement of the individual away from social space and towards the inner space of the self, to a silent conversation about its experience of things, is the origin of every change in the world: from new personal projects of individuals, to the adaptation of common ways of speaking, to a revolution against the entire social order. The moral person is the living threat to every social order and its institutions, and therefore its only legitimate legislator.

People of integrity are therefore unpopular. Every social order is in principle opposed to the moral person who threatens its stability; Ralph Waldo Emerson (in the sexist terms of his day) sees this as a true "conspiracy" of everyone against everyone else: "Society everywhere is in conspiracy against the manhood of every one of its members. […] The virtue in most request is conformity. Self-reliance is its aversion. Society loves not realities and creators, but names and customs."

Every social order stands in the way of reflection, the life element of the moral person, and can only tolerate it to a limited extent. Critics of its rules, who could possibly lead others to the stupid idea of moral objection, have been marginalized, discredited and, wherever feasible, punished with death by the ruling classes throughout known history. It is always a matter of maintaining the existing order and power structure *through the conformism of the subjects ruled by it.*

How functionaries die

Morality and social conformity are extremes between which we have to balance our lives. At the pole of morality we find the example of ethically remarkable people who, following their moral insight, rejected for themselves all the goods of the ruling order to be able to reform it. (It would be misleading to say that ethically remarkable people "sacrificed" everything to their moral insight. For this insight teaches them that the goods provided by and typically sought in their society are not really good and must be overcome. They don't sacrifice themselves, they show others the futility and perhaps the cruelty of *their* idolatry, by rejecting it. *For this* they are ridiculed, despised and persecuted.)

But who do we find at the other end of the continuum, at the pole of conformity? Well, the conformist. But what is a conformist? Certainly not someone who conforms to a certain degree to the customs and requirements of his environment; we all do this, and if for this very reason we were all rightly called "conformists," the term would be superfluous because it would no longer distinguish anything. The conformist must therefore be someone who has deliberately elevated conformity *to the principle* of his thought and behavior - just as we call him a socialist who deliberately makes the social question the principle of his thought and behavior.

Conformists behave in an orderly manner according to purposes and tenets set for them by others and do not question these prescriptions - they *internalize* them. Conformism is purposeful thinking and doing, and this is *not* to be confused with the reflection and action of a moral person. This may appear to be a far-fetched, artificial distinction, but there is a perfectly clear and simple difference here to be observed.

For the purposeful thinking and doing of conformism replays learned patterns and connections of thought and behavior as soon as a key stimulus is received (which is also part of the learned pattern). The key stimulus does not even have to be really present; with a successfully conditioned conformist, the habit of certain associations of memory is enough to trigger entire cascades of behavior.

Good comedians take advantage of this fact when they merely make brief allusions, which are then thought and felt to their inexorable conclusion by the listeners. It is then as if, with the push of a button, a whole train of thought and emotion is set off in us to run its course. This is why politicians and oligarchs of all kinds are constantly and laboriously struggling to establish the 'right' association patterns in all of us: Only in this way is it possible, for example, to initiate wars of aggression with just a few images of a group of people (such as Muslims, Jews or Christians) previously marked in the media as "suspicious" or "evil" to the sounds of ominous background music.

The term 'society' is the name for the structure of established purposes that sets key stimuli for us to react to, thus allowing these to be practiced and recalled. This can be understood as a constant rehearsal of fixed sequences in thinking and doing. Our reliability in these ways of thinking and doing is our ticket to society, our membership. And depending on how humane or inhumane the purposes institutionalized in our society are, we as its members are then habitual fellow benefactors or fellow criminals.

But let's return to the type, to the extreme figure of the conformist: the purpose we obey as conformists is, if we consider the matter carefully, the external will that has set this purpose; this external will is the one we actually obey in our conformity, not our own. To practice conformism means to offer oneself as a servant to the established powers and their representatives, in order to gain the advantages they have to offer us. The conformist is the executor of the established order. The mass of conformists in any society should be viewed as its 'Chief Executive Officer'; these constitute a force infinitely more influential than all the 'CEOs' of of any society's companies and administrations combined.

When we say in general terms that "Society does this or that," we are actually saying "The conformists do this or that"; or even more precisely: "Each of us, as far as we conform, does this or that." One could say, at the risk of philosophical formalism: For a known purpose, people simply think and do what they have learned to think and do. The conformist abandons the reservation of reflection, of quiet conversation, for doing what is customary or obvious for himself and the others around him.

Insofar as we conform, we declare ourselves in agreement. Conformism is the suspension of man as a moral being, the unmaking of man's reflective reservation toward the usual way of the world, and thus his unconditional submission to the reality created by himself and others like him. This is of dramatic consequence. Conformism, in principle, opens the path to complete destruction of everything of human value and of its only creator, of man himself. Amongst themselves, the conformists wield the uncanny power to allow the established system of rule to reign absolute, inhibited, quite literally, by *nothing* and *nobody*. Conformism is the most eminent constructive and destructive force in recorded history.

But if the conformist *simply* thinks and *simply* does as he is told, what exactly is the nature of the reflection and action of the moral person? Reflection is not simple, but deliberately complex thinking; acting is not simple, but deliberately complex doing. In reflection, we process our experience in silent conversation and continue the life journey of our self by affirming and negating, ordering, rejecting, questioning, ignoring, emphasizing and weighting - and also by attending to the emotional effects that our encounters have on us. In addition to such conscious and semi-conscious activity, reflection brings another, consequential factor into play: time.

Just the act of paying attention *again* to what we have felt and thought, of lingering with our impressions, puts them into a constantly finer and more complex relationship to our previous life experience. Our experience is broken up in the course of reflection and brought into a community, into a momentary simultaneity and interaction with ourselves. 'With ourselves' means here: with the thoughts and attitudes that defined us up to the present moment, and with our memory of them.

In reflection, we subject our experience to a comprehensive confrontation with our self, not only intellectually, but also emotionally and affectively. I say that we "subject" our experience to this confrontation because this process does not happen of its own accord by virtue of our sentient existence; we have to reflect on our experience. Our self then *criticizes* our experience on several levels. Intellectually, we allow this or that part of our experience to figure into our silent conversation as a new part of our self-narration, while we ignore or reject other components. Emotionally and affectively, we connect more closely with what seems to us to be pleasant and uplifting, and we intuitively seek to reduce the influence of unpleasant experiences on our inner life.

We thus, in the process of reflecting, also react *organically* to our experience. We are psychosocial systems that have a limited capacity to see, feel and embrace difference, and this is precisely what makes us stable and fit for life. In reflection, we can watch this process of separating, rejecting, embracing and welcoming occur in ourselves, and in doing so, we understand ourselves a little better. Reflecting, we can *see what is happening to us*, that which otherwise *simply happens*, shaping and forming us directly.

It is only through reflection that the experience we encounter becomes *our* experience, the experience of *this* self, *my* experience. It is only through reflection that our experience loses the total, directly formative power over us, which it has first in the experience of the young child and youth and then again in the purpose-driven thinking of conformism.

Reflection is how we can come to discover and define the craft of our lives instead of invariably repeating the given. It allows us to act as ourselves, instead of simply doing what others have taught us - and this precisely because reflection and understanding are powerless in the world - at least *immediately* powerless. The insight that our reflection brings about in the light of our experience is without consequence except within me, indeed, in the development of my own understanding. Only because it is powerless and without consequences can it remain *outside* existing lines of conflict and thus question, enlighten and, if necessary, reject everything that claims validity.

To assume the standpoint of critique (i.e., of discernment) means to leave aside the struggle to achieve this or that effect in the world, in favor of understanding and judging. At the end of a process of understanding, practical demands may come to mind that can enable us to escape the spell of the established purposes of our membership in society - that is, practical demands that move beyond the simple thinking and simple doing of conformism. Simple thinking and simple doing, however, is always oriented toward achieving something specific from the outset, and therefore it cannot provide me any insight into what I *should* think and do.

Conformism is the fulfillment of established purposes. Conformism can therefore only recite what is already known, already thought and already done, and use that purposefully. The simple thinking and doing of the conformist is incapable of recognizing something new as such, and it does not allow for the known to be understood differently than before. For simple thinking, the new is either an error or an absurdity; for the simple doing of conformism, a novelty is a disturbance.

For each individual, his level of conformity is the indicator of his moral vulnerability. With the conformist, the self becomes weak - his will and thus his ability to process his own experience through reflection weakens. His morality, the reservation of reflection against doing the obvious or the customary, is not cultivated. And so, with each year of simply going along, his own fate to exist mainly as a functionary is consolidated. Whatever is original, personal in the life of our mind, is displaced by the habit of yielding to the pressure of outside expectations *often only suspected*, in order to gain what the established order has to offer.

All of us, insofar as we are conformists, are engaged in a certain sport: that of anticipating outside expectations. If we have guessed correctly a few times and had luck with the momentary tactical behavior we ended up choosing, we will remember these successful speculations. They become the basis of our usual expectations, what the others probably expect - our 2nd order expectations, or, as Niklas Luhmann puts it in an untranslatable term, our "Erwartungserwartungen" (*expectation-expectations, or expectations of expectations*). As we move through society, we refer to this past training in the sport of conformity to decide how we should strive to appear to others in this or that situation, in order to advance our pre-conceived interests.

Being conformist is therefore a complicated, time- and energy-consuming matter, and it by no means represents the famous 'path of least resistance.' One tries to credibly display on the outside an inner life that was studiously simulated according to the imagined expectations and likings of others. The sport of conformity is training in self-estrangement. This is precisely the program that *every* society has in store for us: the abolition of our own reflection in favor of an anticipatory obedience that speculates about probable outside expectations. This is the stunting of our self, the abolition of our own normative perspective on the world.

What remains is a human being operating strictly on the outside, one who, without delay or inner complication, reacts to incoming stimuli through appropriate processing in simple thinking and doing. The conformist thus executes the existing order seamlessly, without interposed reflection that might compromise efficient operation of established systems. As Theodor W. Adorno says, the conformist "collaborates with the world in his own defeat." This timeless type of man is the functionary whose narrative of himself is simply and directly determined by the prevailing facts and generally accepted external demands. It is this thoughtless clarity that so appalls Harry Mulisch and Hannah Arendt in their otherwise very different reports on the Jerusalem trial of Nazi criminal Adolf Eichmann.

Functionaries, people of thoughtless clarity and directness, are the best support and the preferred educational outcome of *any* ruling order and *any* organization: For they are generally of a happy disposition and morally undemanding - at least until the moment when someone does not want to play along in their own career advancement or simply in preserving their comfortably numb state of mind. Then, however, such functionaries tend to be very sensitive to the perceived injustices to which they feel themselves subjected.

This type of thoughtless, opportunistic, boundlessly self-righteous functionary is the starting point for investigating and understanding the apparently incomprehensible horrors that people have caused others to suffer with industrial consistency. At the same time, the influence of functionaries is also indispensable to the spread and maintenance of the enormous human achievements of the modern world. For conformist spirits are all the more reliable in operation. Nothing stands in the way of their blind obedience, i.e., their 'professionalism'.

Anyone who is not thoughtless enough for an industrious career as a functionary - for example, due to excess intellectual interests or education - represents an irritation for any system. The functionaries and dignitaries of the various apparatuses have then to put up with his thoughts and questions and live in fear that he might "do something" that is uncoordinated with their standard interests.

But luckily, the establishment has an offer of reconciliation even for notorious intellectuals and naysayers – it offers them a second chance, an alternative educational path into life as a functionary. Where resources permit and the investment promises a positive return, the delinquent is gladly assigned a coach - i.e., a discussion partner with whom one clarifies what kind and what sequence of compromises with the conformists will be *just about* permissible by one's own integrity.

At the first meeting, the coach says: "It is not about changing you as a personality. It's simply a matter of expanding your behavioral repertoire." Translation to reality: "Your personality, actually *any consideration of anyone's personal traits*, is completely irrelevant to the business of career success. This is about making you an athlete of situational conformism."

The probing, creative work of reflection that makes the moral person is suspended by conformism. The functionary replaces it by invoking and following existing authority. We are all affected by this whenever we forget ourselves to perform a function. Our work on our self, which is life itself, rests in these moments. Not only the moral person, the self, is a victim of conformism. Moreover, in both our own reflections and exchanges with others, reality is pushed out of sight by conformism.

Reality falls by the wayside because purposeful reflection can only perceive it in a distorted form. Our presupposed goal and interest orders the picture of reality we create for ourselves: the caricature of our situation that emerges in this way is entirely determined by our subjective goals and the means to achieve them.

Reflecting on our experience alone leads us to productive engagement with that which we have encountered; only where we reflect are we moral beings who judge everything by their own measure, ensuring that we do not simply accept or even glorify what we find. Without reflection, we function for others. Where we act as functionaries, our personality is not present; where we *habitually* act as functionaries and no longer notice this, we are, so to speak, dead in a living body: We can no longer return to a self-determined life because we don't see that we have abandoned it.

How people stay alive

In the particular manner required by our particular biography, we struggle with good reason against this tendency of our membership in society. Nobody wants to consciously concede the reservation one has, owing to their reflection, against doing, to concede one's morality, which is at the same time one's freedom. This sounds abstract, but it immediately becomes concrete when we consider what it actually means to 'give up', or 'concede one's morality.' We could then no longer commune with other people as human beings, but only as functionaries.

Once I surrender my morality, *there is nothing else* between me and other people but one transient social situation after the other, each with its specific expectations of conformity that I may more or less master and fulfill. This emptiness is revealed when functionaries meet after work and their conversation ebbs away in embarrassed silence or seeks refuge in banal and repetitive chatter about the various concerns of their daily grind or compensatory habits of consumption.

Let's sharpen this insight by making another approach from a slightly different angle: Besides the steady sequence of social situations, each with its own respective demands of conformity, over and beyond functioning, what else is it that can possibly exist between people? Well, life: the process of reflecting on our experience, weaving the fruits of that experience into the self, aligning our aspirations with what we consider valuable, and sharing it with others.

In this exchange, a community of people negotiates its identity, its common narrative and, in this sense, its collective self. In a tangle of countless moments of understanding, misunderstanding and sheer communication breakdown, as characterized by the inability to even recognize that the other person is expressing something, let alone to grasp what it is, the intricate web of what is sayable grows in an uncoordinated fashion. At the same time, the community of speakers estab-lishes both that which simply does not occur in its view of the world, and that which – while it may be sensed by some - is unspeakable in a given community.

So it never becomes clear *conclusively and definitively* what it means to be, e.g., a German, a lawyer, a union member, heterosexual or homosexual; but quite a lot of things about it can be said in many combinations and shades. An inescapable vagueness always remains when we try to convey meaning to each other. And the coarse approximations of meanings that we convey to one other and to which we respond in kind, are enough to make us feel part of a world and at home in the web of our language and gestures.

In the course of our exchange with others, this essential vagueness about our actual commonality in each society creates continual uncertainty about the social conditions in which we are living together. (This vagueness corresponds precisely to the particular aspect of self-invention that we experience individually when we philosophize and thereby seek to learn the craft of our lives.)

As members of a community, we grant each other this uncertainty, due to the increased intensity of our attempts to be intelligible, *precisely* when we want to express ourselves clearly to truly be understood. The careful, concentrated use of familiar words, firmly intent to solicit agreement, is the very act that brings the differences in understanding between the interlocutors fully to bear.

This uncertainty about what our *shared* identity is and what it demands, despite all the differences in our histories, is the initial moment of politics. It is present where people meet in reflection, simply because of our constitution as finite beings with a certain position in the continuous connection of all things that limits our insight. Starting from this moment of reflection, by virtue of its force, things can become different than they are; in this moment lies all the vitality of a community (or its lack thereof).

For in reflection with others, we cannot naively conceive of the pre-existing social relations as a set of given and legitimate purposes, and thoughtlessly execute them. In every exchange, we recognize at once that we do not see and understand the same thing, although we want to speak of the same object. Communication stems from a lack of understanding, from the need to achieve, secure and protect shared understandings in order to build on them. Reflecting together with others brings us into contact with their experience and their manner of processing it.

This brings three unpredictable elements into play: the actual experience of the other person, his processing of this experience in the light of what he knew (or thought he knew) up to this point, and, finally, the degree of my own receptiveness to what is being offered. What is certain is that the other person's experience cannot correspond to my own; nor can his previous knowledge match with any exactness my own previous knowledge. And whatever he offers me in our exchange is then caricatured, distorted, parodied or glorified by me through the silent influence of my experience and prior knowledge, and certainly also simplified to what I then *come to understand*.

The social order, in the context of which we speak and have roles of varying influence, allows the more powerful person, the superior, to pass over this fundamental, permanent precarity of communication by simply ordering us to move on to the next agenda item. We do this when we simply think, but not when we reflect on our experience. With the command by the superior to "get on with it," shared reflection is left behind. For this consists precisely in our grasping our dissent with the experience and conclusions of the other, and in our dwelling on them. This is the only process by which the divergent experiences of different individuals can be integrated into a mostly shared apperception of our situation.

Only through the conscious suspension of the structure of social roles and power relations for the duration of our encounter with the other person does exchange with this other person become politics - work on a common identity, on the identity (the self) of a community. In this way, the social order of those speaking becomes for them again what it always has been independently of them - a historically evolved space of characteristic opportunity and limitation in which I myself objectively have meaning and influence, because it was the actions of others like myself that created this historical space. This is the fundamental fact that grounds the philosophical necessity of granting equal rights to everyone in society, something the western constitutional states of the postwar-era are meant to safeguard.

This is how action emerges. First we step out of simple thinking transacted in learned reflexes of obedience to tradition, and we cease to simply do something. Socially, action begins in a thoughtful exchange with others: We suspend our consent to the prevailing conditions that rest and rely on our silence for their force, and begin the work of understanding and politics. For the person who simply thinks and simply does, who thus functions, does not act, but carries out the ruling order; he remains just as he has become - just as he has to be to remain harmless and useful to those in power.

If an individual has been trained to become an envious careerist who traverses a narrow horizon of materially understood self-interests, and who uses his mental powers to 'optimize' his 'shopping experience,' he will in this capacity ruin the world. He will also not seek politics, i.e., he will be disinterested in reaching an understanding with others about their experience and in arriving at shared conclusions ultimately expressed in joint political action. Instead, he will remain "imperially alone" (David Foster Wallace), and his society will simply continue until "the last ton of coal has burned up," as Max Weber gloomily puts it.

Neither for himself nor with others is this man able to reform anything; the ruling authority is served, what is considered rational or even reasonable in his surroundings is propagated into the future, and nothing can change. This state, not the final cessation of our heartbeat, is tantamount to death, the final petrifaction of a being that is not only able to think but to reflect, and that is therefore not only subject to its acquired conditioning and social situation, but also, through its actions, its own creator.

Every society, by virtue of its unavoidable pressures to conform, sets its individuals on this path to moral abdication. To avoid following this path blindly to its fatal endpoint of lifeless functioning, is the personal task of each individual, in every society. Everything that is humanly important and a potential hindrance to the functioning of our society, asserts itself in this struggle of the individual. Otherwise, it comes to an end with the loss of morality - with the abandonment of our reflective reservation against doing. Conformism drives us to extinguish our personal life as moral beings in the pursuit of security, i.e., of a function, for us.

4 The order of prestige

Every society forces its members into the individual struggle both for moral integrity and against the necessity of adaptation. What is special about the industrial society of our time is the variety of forms and the graded degrees of violence with which it pushes us onto the path of the functionary. It ensures that the cheerful and efficient pursuit of any purpose, that is, that a morally unscrupulous pragmatism of the functionary becomes the dominant mentality - and that most victims of this mentality and its consequences do not develop any awareness of the problem.

This, our present-day reality, has a long prehistory marked by the systematic weakening of independent reflection and thereby also the moral person. This prehistory explains how nowadays the individual's moral disenfranchisement and practical integration into industrial society can succeed almost comprehensively. As we now attempt to account for this development, a certain change of pace as compared to that in the previous chapters is required: We are now thinking in terms of the history of ideas, with the aim of understanding our present-day situation, starting from its base principles.

Our self-evident principles and their predecessors

A type of social discipline that robs people of their reflection and transforms them into functionaries must go largely unnoticed in order to remain unchallenged. Only one species of logic can manage to go undisputed: it must be present in everything that is said and done. Only in this way can it reliably remain hidden.

The historical basis of industrial society must lie in a combination of feelings and thoughts without which we cannot understand our reflections and actions - and which we usually do not consider taken in isolation by themselves. In short, we must identify what is 'self-evident' in our culture. For only what is supposedly self-evident and what therefore remains undiscussed, really wields complete and unchallenged power over us. And once we notice what it is that has us in its power, many other problems take care of themselves. Seen in this light, what are the self-evident thoughts, behaviors, institutions of our day that explain the devastating disciplinary success of industrial society?

Any answer to this question is contestable with sound reasons. Several profound, coherent responses are conceivable, each of which begins from a different intellectual vantage point. But this is not a problem and does not pose any objection to the attempt at an explanation undertaken here. It is obvious that several self-evident things have over time become elementary to our present: the monetary economy, trade and the division of labor would be materially-oriented examples; in the spiritual realm, one can think, among other things, of individualism, juridification, and the addiction to fill the space of freedom with nothing (i.e., to seek entertainment). Based on each of these self-evident facts, one can write cultural diagnoses and cultural critiques of our present era, which rightly criticize the fact that these factors rule our lives as a matter of course and therefore completely unhindered.

In my opinion, however, there is one factor in our cultural history that has established itself as self-evident and that allows both more concrete and more general insights than the other candidates for self-evident principles. This factor lies hidden in plain sight, and it constantly guides and restricts us. Its outer shell practically forms the everyday suit of our self, so to speak: This factor is our concept of honor - as understood simply in the sense of prestige or status. Hence, we concentrate on what can be called external or formal honor.

Why should we give the externally understood concept of honor such a central role in the analysis of ourselves and our present? Isn't it a trivial truth that at all times people orient themselves in relation to the presumed expectations of others in order to elevate or at least secure their social status? Yes: "Man often lives with himself and needs virtue, and lives with others and needs honor" (Nicolas Chamfort), this is nothing new. And it is also true that rooted deep in our history, there are many concepts of honor that, far from being matters of merely external prestige, are morally rich; one need only think of the almost proverbial concepts of chivalry, the honorable merchant, the medieval craft guilds, or religiously-based ideas such as the active charity of a Christian.

In the second chapter we conducted a general discussion of the direct, practical meaning of the values that close-knit communities with a shared ethos could reliably convey to their members. We also discussed there the peculiar distance we modern people have to the values that guide our actions. For with industrialization and anonymous mass society, an epoch has arisen in which explicitly and richly articulated moral models have lost much of their integrating power. They have become milieu concepts that are not suitable for holding society as a whole together.

An outward sense of honor in status or prestige - "an enigmatic mixture of conscience and selfishness" (Jacob Burckhardt) - is the means of social integration that remained after this historical development. We play a positioning game with each other that is oriented on outward appearances, not on moral content. In modern times, the reciprocal demonstration and deprivation of honor in this external sense of status and prestige, has gained fundamental importance for the stability of society - precisely to the extent that once generally binding ideals have split into quarrelsome factions and faded from our common consciousness. This is why our diagnosis of the present focuses on honor in the sense of a person's status and prestige, as seen in the eyes of the other members of society.

In order to better understand this conceptual starting point, we take the time to remind ourselves of the culture preceding the modern era in Europe. Let us listen for a moment to the historian of ideas

Will-Erich Peuckert, who describes the medieval order as a world built on what he calls "peasant thinking":

> *Being a peasant was God's command to mankind when he pushed Adam out of paradise [...]. In ancient times, the ancestral sagas in the Bible were still accepted as an indispensable, serious truth, as Berthold of Regensburg, the great preacher, regarded every true work, "the builder's work in his building, the merchant's work in his purchase, the craftsman's work in his trade, the knight's work in his knighthood," as a peasant's work. Not only 'man' is ultimately a "peasant", all categories of his life, whether it is birth or death or marital work, receive their meaning from this. Peasant thinking and the life of the peasants [determined] everything. The king of the Middle Ages was a peasant king. A pater familias (in the sense of a family head; note Andrick) is the king, and a pater familias is the god of medieval man.*

Peuckert further depicts the despair of contemporaries in the medieval Holy Roman Empire of the German Nation in a way that is both vivid and worth reading: the repeated attempts at "imperial reform" by emperors and clergy long before Luther's actual reformation, the myths and fantasies of the "good emperor" who would rise from the dead for the final battle and restore a just balance. All this is the expression of disappointments caused a peasant population by concrete persons because they did not seem to fulfill the duties prescribed for them in the divine world order.

In the Middle Ages, love, loyalty and service personal affairs, transacted among people who could conceive of themselves as part of the same divine order; and so, naturally, also the despair over the failure of that order was always inspired by, and attached to, particular people. Hopes for betterment and relief are not directed towards new ideas or principles as in later revolutions - but towards individuals who would finally do justice again to their God-given role, for the good of all.

But these hopes are in vain, the community and ancient imagery of peasant life has been eroded and vanquished in the course of time.

The 'good faith' that was supposed to govern relations in the old, divinely instated fiefdom has been lost, overstretched, and worn out by technical and social developments. The great discoveries at the turn of the 16th century - America, the printing press, double-entry bookkeeping in the merchant community, the sea route to India, and the further exploration of the oceans - were not driven by peasant, but by urban civil, often commercial interests; for Peuckert, these interests represent the dawning of modernity.

The specific character of peasant thinking, which formed the basis of pre-modern communities and social life, had nothing at all to do with these new interests. The oath of personal loyalty sworn to a certain soil had become impotent to banish the evil spirits of disorder - especially since it could now also be the case that the one to whom one swore his oath belonged to a different denomination of the fragmented Christian faith than one's own neighbor and his prince.

Isaac Bashevis Singer lets Esriel, the apostate young rabbi in his novel *The Manor*, utter a telling sigh that sums up the epochal changes of the Renaissance and Reformation 300 years later, and that evokes the perplexity that is still with us today: "He had renounced God, but was dependent on all sorts of bureaucrats. Esriel felt that he had made a mistake. But what exactly had been his mistake? How could it be made right?" Nothing can be "made right" here; we pay for our disagreement on ideological issues to this day and irrevocably with an anonymization of the structures of our social reality.

Norbert Elias has characterized the development, which saw the network of close-knit communities with a shared world of ideas described by Peuckert become an anonymous mass society, as a process of steadily increasing discipline. The emerging central states divorce power relations from the personal level, from the direct relationship between people known to one another, and draw those power relations into the impersonal realm of structure, of an administrative apparatus. This creates a new social playing field; it becomes a practical necessity for the individual to orientate himself to the presumed demands of anonymous others and of the administrative apparatus that now rules over him.

In the Middle Ages, the reason for a person's honor or disgrace was their fulfillment or disregard of their God-given function in the community. Today, my gain or loss of reputation is accounted for in terms of my fulfillment or disregard of the role in society imagined for me by other people. Our existence is now no longer communal and concrete, but societal and abstract. And it is precisely this development and dynamic that puts the concept of honor, understood in its outward, superficial sense of prestige and status, at the center of attention.

However, the concrete ideas of honor held by the medieval states and associations, all deeply shaped by the Christian faith, continue to resonate when we speak of honor today, when we praise or rebuke one another in social exchange. The prestige of ideas like chivalry, of the Honest Merchant or the Good Christian, still in part determines what we feel, think and say about our own and other people's behavior.

But these concepts of honor and shame, rich in moral detail and steeped as they are in spiritual associations, can no longer serve as a means of coordination in a society that is divided into social classes and ideological milieus. In this historical situation, we therefore focus on the collective game in which we grant each other status and prestige, or, in degrees, withhold respect. It is from this perspective that we can now decipher our entire moral order, the manner and the prevailing atmosphere of our social existence.

The pressure of centuries

The exact elucidation of this modern order of prestige, which is an order based on the mutual regard that people show for one another in social space, will take some effort; its inner workings are somewhat complex. But understanding those opens up broad far-reaching insights The horizon of inquiry and understanding that we want to reach with the following considerations has been explored by Hannah

Arendt in her writings on evil. In these texts she discusses the Third Reich at length.

What she found enigmatic and astounding about Hitler's dictatorship and its crimes was not that there were fanatical anti-Semites, sadists and other mentally disturbed people who committed the worst of crimes against defenseless victims. Morally, Arendt was not interested in the blind "ideological fanatic" or the common criminal. In her opinion, a certain number of such figures could be found at any time and in any society; and they would always stand at the ready to execute any ruling ideology, no matter how absurd and inhuman.

For Arendt, the riddle lay in those who "merely conformed and did not act out of conviction" - and in the astonishingly seamless retransformation of these perpetrators into inconspicuous citizens after the total defeat of Germany. In his grueling, indispensable play *Der Stellvertreter* (*The Deputy*), Rolf Hochhuth vividly described such cases, for example a "Scharführer of the Waffen-SS," Sergeant Witzel: "The rude, obscene, inanely loquacious tone which he adopts towards Jews and other defenseless people (since that just is how you speak to such people), does not suit him very well. Without realizing it, Witzel has taken over this brutal jargon, even whole sentences of it, from his superior as quickly as he will get rid of it once his superior has changed. He is a reliable citizen in 1959." In the stage directions for his play, Hochhuth remarks that the actor impersonating Witzel should play a priest and a Jewish policeman in other scenes - "one should not even stick a fake beard on him when he changes roles."

This book works on the same mystery that occupied Arendt and that Hochhuth so depressingly illustrated; our question at the beginning of the opening chapter was: How does industrial society achieve our conformism - our practically unconditional striving, to any conceivable end? Depressingly few people who were under the influence of modern administrations maintained moral independence in the mass crimes and wars of the 20th century. Can we manage to do that today?

Our global economic order, together with an undreamt-of gain in prosperity for billions, also causes the human catastrophe of radical inequality and ecological crises; there is, thus, today an entire professional field in the non-governmental sector that discusses this order as an institutionalized crime, and for reasons that can hardly be dismissed. Jean Ziegler, for decades a UN functionary, describes the current situation in his last book as a "cannibalistic world order." I attribute these phenomena to the fact that at the beginning of the 20th century, a certain form of social pressure to conform had already been effective for centuries; it is precisely this particular manifestation and logic of social conformation that I call the order of prestige.

It is characteristic at least for the European-American cultural tradition; with a view to other parts of the world, I cannot judge. This particular system of turning us away from reflection, of constant distraction from building and caring for the self, has grown historically, establishing and fortifying itself continuously. The mass army, the mass party, mass organizations in general are the product and expression of the order of prestige; the characteristic feature of all of these is the perfectly engineered external direction of individuals and the simultaneous elimination of their moral independence, by steering them away from critical reflection.

The fact that mass organizations could exist at all and that they had a significant historical impact shows that the weakening and often destruction of the moral identity of modern man by the order of prestige had preceded them. The institutions that make mass crimes organizable are effective because they can base their calculations on the mentality of the modern conformist. Hitler, for example, after the *Machtergreifung* (seizure of power) did not have to manipulatively impose the necessary conformism on a people of intact moral persons. The Germans, like other modern people and like us today, were already culturally trained to be conformists.

Imagine the future as the result of a network of current events that allows certain developments and excludes others from the realm of possibilities. Industrially organized mass crimes as well as the planned destruction of our planet's ecosystem were included as real possibilities in the web of historical conditions since the dawn of the European modern age. Their occurrence does not mean that human history enters a new epoch with these crimes, but that it has culturally developed a possibility over a long period of time, that is now being realized. As far as the fundamental conceptual changes are concerned, the epochal turning point occurred long before the appearance of a new type of crimes and criminals, by which colonial political genocides or the Holocaust could be carried out.

Do we have reason to doubt that political leadership could have used the German Reichswehr and public administration to commit mass murder of a specific population group already during the First World War? The ideological preparation of the general population for such an endeavor could also have been executed earlier and in other countries. If the mining technique of "Mountaintop Removal" (which blows up whole mountains to exploit ores and leaves behind a lunar landscape and water contamintted with heavy metals) had been known 200 years ago, the mountains would have been blown up 200 years ago. The institutions of industrial society, with their inner dynamism of bold, mindless conformism, are the product of the historically deep-rooted order of prestige, which is completely devoid of concrete moral content. They place the enormous mobilization potential of this mentality at the disposal of any leader or party that appears on the scene with power and just minimal psychological skill.

Communication breakdown

A logic of status and ambition orders our behavior and explains our specifically modern fate; yet its omnipresence renders it largely invisible. This is why this logic has a thousand friends and very effective defenders: because established thinking proceeds according to the conceptual patterns of honor and ambition, any attempt to make this logic as such the object of investigation must break with established patterns of both thought and speech. This must present us with communication problems. Because, as David Foster Wallace notes, fish know nothing about water and will react to a lecture on the subject with a shrug.

What is seen as self-evident is not usually discussed. So in order to name and question the status quo, I have to speak in a way that is difficult to understand. It is therefore sufficient for any conformist of the existing order to point this out and ask "What do you actually want to say?" To which I must then reply: "Nothing that our language is set up to express, but precisely that which it is best suited to conceal." For every truly fundamental error, i.e., every error that founds a whole society, has as its accomplice an entire language - after all, only the understanding of things that prevails in and through our language is considered common sense.

To advance in this exploration, we must first of all find a language that breaks through our self-understanding - that gives us an outside view of our industrial existence. We recognize such a language by the fact that it alienates us, that it makes it difficult for us to understand, and that its use in front of others leaves us feeling uncomfortable, perhaps embarrassed.

For we understand others and things from within our industrial existence. Our words, gestures, questions and answers, our understanding of others, and the social recognition of ourselves are all based on the language cultivated in the interior space of our industrial existence; language both represents and affirms, supports and reproduces this interior space. This language is the dwelling place of our thoughts and feelings today, which was mentioned at the beginning of the second chapter.

To depart from this language even partially is implies a renunciation of loyalty to that which supposedly unites us, to that which creates and maintains a home in the world for us together with others. Every change requires this renunciation of agreement, which will always be perceived by some as an attack. Texts addressing fundamental errors are an imposition on our habitual thinking and on the language that we use and that guides us; they extend an invitation to understand ourselves and everything around us differently than before. Only claims that are far-fetched and that stretch the realm of our imagination beyond its usual limits have any chance at all of reaching "the hearts of the prevailing shadows" (Paul Celan). Other theses do not even attempt to do so because they are launched from a point of view that is too close to this heart and that is itself therefore obscured.

In our case, the required language is a new and different idiom about life, self, philosophy, morality and conformity, honor, ambition, work and the world of work, and the distorted form of humanity cultivated in it. At this point of reflection, we are already in the midst of an effort to alienate ourselves from our habitual use of these terms, to postpone or completely redefine their application. For only in this way can these terms become the tool of a new understanding of our life situation. The new way of speaking then requires a certain degree of habituation until it no longer seems ridiculous or abstruse.

Some of the challenges posed by the new language have already been mentioned and may have annoyed or irritated some readers; e.g., that many people in industrial society do not lead a life, but only execute a function. (Siegfried Kracauer already formulated this dark presumption, "that under the present economic and social conditions, people do not live life," prior to the Second World War). Says the conformist: "But living means following the rules of the game and buying a home. Just do it." The insight toward which this and the next chapters are driving - that the core virtue of the industrial and competitive society, ambition, plays a key role in thwarting our lives – will ring equally absurd at first. Again the conformist: "But what if my ambition is to be the best of all Christians? What's wrong with that?"

Many do not actually lead a life, and ambition plays an essential role in this context: If these two assertions, to which for the moment we let the conformists respond unchallenged, then the self-image of our society is unrealistic. For the guiding principle of the German constitution and other Western charters of basic rights is the "free development of personality." State institutions are supposed to guarantee and make this possible in practice. This is what we learn in school, and the heroes of our television series are therefore also people who seem able in one way or another to succeed in this enterprise of self-realization.

Accordingly, the normal self-understanding held by the members of our society is that we lead a life of our own design - and that our success in doing so depends very much on our ambition. Even this individual variation of our social self-image must be unrealistic if the analyses developed in this book on the fate of the functionary and the specific madness of ambition (which are yet to come) are correct. In fact, this unrealistic self-conception has become especially entangled with the problem of ambition, because our belief in self-made success legitimizes ambition as a virtue. Nothing, we shall see later, is morally more dangerous than this error of judgment.

It should therefore come as no surprise at all if the philosophically, stepwise 'reformed' language of this book were to cause offense and provoke rejection. The analysis of our present, toward which I am working with this language, contradicts the established "common sense," which I believe leads us astray. The disease of the world is always the "common sense" of society. No other pathogen would affect the whole organism and would be omnipotent to destroy it.

We can only escape the blindness that every engrained way of thinking brings with it, through enlightenment in the full sense of that term: through historically informed, open-minded reflection and inquiry. Thinking historically means assuming that what we know has emerged from something else; thinking in an enlightened way means acknowledging and always bearing in mind that our own point of view is bound up with concepts that have themselves a history of human interest, error and aspiration; a history that includes our personal biases and predilections.

By no means do our concepts simply act as "honest brokers," together uniting the thinker with his object of attention. Hence, the question arises for us: Exactly what combination of new experience and previously established ways of thinking engendered in our history was it that positioned the concepts of status and ambition to order our lives from the ground up? We start by first thinking about the concept of honor in terms of status or prestige in the eyes of others, and then proceed to examine ambition, as well, in the chapters that follow.

The social framework of honor

It is difficult to talk about the concept of honor, because that which concerns and touches everything is hard to identify and bring into focus. Its omnipresence is what keeps it hidden. The role and power of the concept of honor, status and prestige in the fabric and business of our lives are difficult to determine because it is ubiquitous in our habitual thinking, speaking and behavior, thus not appearing at all as such, or in isolation.

Rather, the concept of honor rules directly over us: Understood in its thin, external sense of status or prestige, it is the central structure of modern society and the associated consciousness; it is not a part of this structure ("a supporting pillar," "a decisive factor," or something of the like).

All attempts to justify public order by reference to God's will or other points of reference beyond our experience have failed. This undertaking only lives on as more or less successful warfare against supposedly "unenlightened" people; at present, for example, as Islamist terror, which provides the US military empire and its entourage with the pretext for wars of aggression and extra-legal killing campaigns.

It took European-influenced culture centuries to learn this lesson, but it is clear now: Without the concept of honor as the ordering spirit and structuring mechanism of behavior, a public order that is by and large reliable would be unthinkable. And what is unthinkable cannot be established in a planned fashion: We can indeed cause all kinds of errors and confusion with our concepts, but we cannot step out of the framework set by them.

Therefore, with the development of the following reflections, we will become certain of living situated within the framework of the concept of honor, and about knowing and using the thinking and language of this environment and no other. To inquire after the terms "honor," "prestige" or "status," means thus to ask ourselves directly what kind of social being we have learned to be. There is no smaller, more modest scope of inquiry open to us at this point. So let us draw a panorama of our past and present, starting from, and building on, the modern concept of honor.

The concept of honor of a society summarizes what makes a person a good cooperative partner measured by its conceptions of value. These conceptions of value of a society are, in part, explicitly formulated and explained, for example in a constitution. But equally important are the unwritten rules that are simply practiced. The concept of honor in a given era is the epitome of what is usually praised or rebuked in a society. Those who want recognition must consider this code and adhere to its requirements.

In this sense, a change in the form of society is always also the replacement of one concept of honor by another; "good cooperation" is understood differently in a nomadic society than in a sedentary one, and differently in a socialist society than in a capitalist one. To this day, 30 years after reunification, the interpersonal manners of East German and West German people are often different. East Germans have mostly learned to make little fuss about themselves in their community, because this corresponded to the official socialist ideology with its emphasis on the collective. West Germans, on the other hand, were mostly prepared for self-assertion in competition, because this corresponded to the official ideology of the capitalist, competitive market economy.

My personal honor, my social status is the barometer of my adaptation to the expectations of my society; and the others take their reading of it constantly. My social status is never precisely discernible and keeps my appraisers and myself in constant uncertainty. On the one hand, the mercury in this barometer is constantly rising or falling, depending on who is with me; on the other hand, the scale of the barometer can never be fixed with accuracy. For my society's concrete expectations of conformity are constantly evolving in the light of new experience. At some point, it had become acceptable for the majority to take out their mobile phones and send text messages during a personal conversation.

The people who represent society for me in a concrete situation always bring their very personal interpretations and expectations into play. There is also a necessary degree of speculation on the part of my cooperation partners: Every human self is unique and unrepeatable because every individual life experience is unique and unrepeatable. Therefore, any assessment of myself from the outside is by its nature very approximate and limited. As they dose their tributes to me, they decide under uncertainty.

Our discourse of honor is a vague business, driven by suppositions and intuitions. But still we cannot do without it. Our talk about prestige and status marks the act of imagining and judging each other, without which a group of people cannot cohere as a society. Only by means of this guesswork and judgement about whether someone helps to realize the value concepts of the community or harms them can these standards be enforced and the community be maintained.

The concept of honor is the tool by which respect is shown for the views of others, but not only for the views of others. For our views inform our wills when we try to assert our conceptions of value. Therefore, the concept of honor is our cultural means of demonstrating respect for the other person's will, for the value concepts of others, and therefore it is our cultural means of respecting them. By applying the equally extensive, infinitely complex and often hidden set of rules for honoring our fellow human beings - from rituals of welcome to the exercise of tact in communicating our ideas and representing our interests -, we constantly show that other people's thoughts and volitions are acknowledged and considered by us to be practically important.

The rules of courtesy and etiquette are usually observed without us making the slightest concession to others in the assertion of our competences. In reality, our actions show that we are mostly indifferent to the opinions and wishes of others. Nevertheless, doing what we are entitled to do, or just want to do, loses its social legitimacy if we disregard the ritual of showing respect to others in some recognizable fashion.

Although our dealings entail a constant consideration of others' perspectives, of their value concepts and their will, this way of dealing is not an expression of constant subordination or even submission to their points of view. We know of funny or tragic situations of 'fiddling about' in which people find themselves unable to make a decision, out of endless consideration for the presumed sensitivities of others - but these occasions are rather rare. A culture of all-round giving in would have the absurd consequence that no decisions could ever be reached - because apart from cases where a compromise is factually possible, every decision between alternatives represents the assertion of one point of view over another.

A literal interpretation of our all-sided, continuous ritualism of respect as being completely authentic and truthful in its intent to accept others, has absurd consequences. Also, the softer interpretation, namely, that the general ritualism of respect is at least more often than not a sign of the actual acknowledgement of views or intentions expressed by others, does not stand up to scrutiny. Every society is a power structure that counts on the regularity of the actions occurring within it. Its statics would never be stable if it were dependent on the possibly short-term shifts in the prevailing views and desires of some members of society. With our constant bows to each other, we merely demonstrate that we respect the other person as an equal counterpart in principle, that is, that we take him into account.

In conclusion, we must infer that our ritualism of respect for others is concerned with their value concepts and views only on a very superficial reading. And something else is clear: we cannot interpret the peculiar dance of honoring each other that we perform with one other socially exclusively as a simple routine of maintaining our status in the eyes of the others. In a mobile mass society, the others can easily be different people in every situation we encounter. So why do we live with, or even in, a complex ritualism by which one another's significance is externally recognized? After all, we know when performing these rituals that we cannot authentically have the others in mind, and that they will only very rarely become our permanent cooperation partners.

Respect as a cult of authority

Our behavior can be understood as a cult of authority, as a constitutional ritual. It is the expression of a learned mentality that stabilizes our order of values. The constant bow to each other in the choice of our words and in our manners is the recognition that our society and my powers in it are based on declarations of will that human persons have made. Our constitutions are self-written, not dictated by God.

Only in this way do these norms have a comprehensible, justifiable authority, namely my authority: Constitutions are the result of a human declaration of will that expresses human value concepts. The source of all norms under which a person could legitimately come to live is present in every human being; the sovereign in this sense is me as a human person. The will of man is the sovereign of modern times, and every sovereign must demand constant formal recognition in order to develop and sustain real power over social life.

This cult does not seem to be a "western," "occidental," or otherwise regionally definable specialty, although I cannot judge this with certainty. In my experience, however, international encounters between people from industrialized societies are always concerned with but the way in which outward reverence is to be paid to members of a particular nation. Yet there is no question that a routine for maintaining visible status is fundamental for exchange and cooperation between as well as for the stability within each of these different societies. *That the human will is the modern sovereign, remains beyond question. And what is beyond question is taken for granted and thus creates social reality.*

This is the basis of the great persuasive power, indeed, the irrefutability of the modern demand for political equality of all people - of an equality organized by law, which emphatically does *not* concern itself with the actual diversity of people. Together we recognize the supremacy of the human will over everything; and because we all possess that will ourselves, no one can legitimately claim power over us to whom we have not given it ourselves.

The idea of political representation of many people by a few whom they themselves have elected for this purpose is the logical consequence of this insight. It is even more consistent to realize the highest possible degree of direct democracy. The demand for political equality for all is rooted in the fundamental moral logic of our age, and therefore it is the fundamental moral and political injustice of modernity not to fulfill this demand.

Representative or better still direct democracy is the only form of government that can be justified for the realization of a culture in which people recognize themselves as masters of all things. The legitimacy of a democratic government lies in the alignment of government action with the intentions of the people - not with the ideas of their representatives. In the Federal Republic of Germany, every member of parliament represents the whole people, regardless of where and for which party he was elected. My representative in parliament is occupied full-time respecting my will, since I (at least in theory) empower him to exercise it for me. The ritualism of bowing to other people's will, which permeates our culture, is always at the same time a confirmation of the importance of my will.

'Honor' in the sense of prestige or status is the cipher, the 'password' for the modern social order; it is the name for its principle. Here, 'principle' has its true double meaning: 'honor' refers to the body of thought from which the modern social order of industrial society unfolded, and 'honor,' in the sense of reputation and status, also refers to the way it functions. Without the final stone of the concept of honor, the vault of our manners would collapse.

A social order based on human power needs the ritualism, the coordination logic of the mutual paying of respect. What people want must have visible importance among them, and that is exactly what the concept of honor ensures. It is the logical means, i.e., the means that regulates our speech and behavior, of showing practical respect to the sovereign – to our will and the institutions it has legitimized - and of keeping this respect alive.

Ascribed Personality

This central importance of our external concept of honor for the culture of our age becomes clear in another way when we look at the process of personality formation. It takes place under difficult conditions. Our society does not provide a specific place, a specific meaning, a specific function for each thing and each person from the very moment it comes into being, as Peuckert explained to us about medieval society: there is no unchanging role, no fate understood as simply given, that fixes for us people and things in the world.

Individuals and groups of people may think differently. Some may be convinced that there is a reason for our existence that extends back behind the world of our experience, such as God or an all-embracing nature, viewed as a spiritual essence of things. Perhaps this Absolute - that is, the unconnected that connects everything - then creates for these people a sense of the unity of all things. But as a collective within certain spatial boundaries - as a society -, we do not think like this: there are many worldviews coexisting. That is why we cannot live together according to rules that presuppose inspiration by absolute instances.

Thus, in the vital business of forming our personal identity, we can only work with what others tell us or otherwise communicate to us through their behavior. The attributions to me of some or other qualities by other people are the only material from which I can form my narrative about myself, i.e., from which I can shape my identity. The sum of these attributions determines the kind of personality someone can become. First of all, it is the pre-conscious acceptance of the attributions of others that lays the foundation for our personality, as psychological attachment research has long shown.

Later in life, the conscious processing of these external attributions is added and completes the picture. During the biographical period before full critical self-reflection, the confirmation and sustenance of a personality formed in this way can only come from others. It is precisely this fact that is both condensed and named in the modern concept of personal honor. In English, the corresponding term 'reputation' still refers directly back to the Latin verb "reputare," which means to attribute or ascribe.

My personal honor is my social shadow: The light that others cast on me determines the outline of this shadow, and its depth indicates to me the area of my carefree security in dealing with others. 'Status' or 'reputation' are appropriate terms for this secure personal space. Our personal honor, our prestige, is not fixed once and for all, but has at all times the character of an assumption, a hypothesis of other people about us. The others who assess my behavior and thus give me my reputation must speculate about my previous experience. Those who want to 'grab me by my honor,' in other words, those who want to take advantage of the strengths and weaknesses of my status, must understand in general terms what norms I have grown accustomed to as binding in the past.

Anyone who wants to praise or criticize my behavior and thus exert influence upon me must start from my biographical background, from my experience. The second hypothetical moment lies with myself. I must speculate about the expectations my fellow human beings have of my thinking and behavior if I want to establish, maintain and develop my status in this society. Who I am, and what role and relative importance I have in society, is the product of two factors: first, my personal sense of honor, which guides my conduct; and then, second, there is that which is actually considered respectable in my society, and that therefore is objectively going to enhance my standing in it.

The social game around prestige and status entails for each individual the solitary exploration of facts that can only be assumed, but not known with certainty. This exploration is focused on the respective will of the others we interact with; a will they may put forward in the polite cult of mutual respect, but that they always want to enforce with or against us. If we look at a single fellow human being, this other will is unclear and can only be estimated with a constant sense of unsurety. This external will appears much clearer, structured and consolidated, where it confronts us in the shape and form of historically evolved institutions which place their demands upon us.

Social Navigation

We cannot escape this adaptation to the sense of honor held by others - firstly, because the only available material for the foundation and stabilization of our personality are the attributions of others to us. On the other hand, we can only solve the vital task of assuming and asserting our own position in the social fabric by constantly paying respect of various kinds and degrees to the will of others.

Whether we succeed in this is determined by the extent to which our moves in this game actually meet the expectations of others. There is no original, person-sensitive honor in public. Just as I cannot decide which behavior is socially tactful or tactless, what I might consider to be laudable cannot be taken as the yardstick of what is honorable - namely, that which is actually praised and rewarded with social status in society. My place in social space is determined only by my successful or unsuccessful addressing and confirming of the actual concept of honor that exists in my society.

In other words, in order to form and maintain my personal identity in a modern society, I must be continually in touch with the anonymous consensus of the wills of others. The ritualism of respect in bourgeois society are rituals that publicly reaffirm a certain pact: We govern ourselves by our own, entirely human will; we may trust other supposed authorities as individuals, but not as a group. For only in this way are we safe from tyrannizing one another in the name of supposedly higher truths.

This navigation of the individual in the web of the presumed views of others is the basic moral reality of modern times. The identity of our society and of its individuals is conceived and maintained by a network of evaluative attributions made between people; each person is a nodal point in this network of fearful acceptance and miserly distribution of honors and shame. Each person stabilizes himself by upholding the others through anticipating and showing obedience to their expectations. Doing this at all, and then, doing it in a more or less skillful way, determines a person's honor - his personal safe space, his reputation, his social status.

In this order of prestige, the takeover of the whole world and all social relations in it by the authority of the human will is expressed. It has an exact and revealing counterpart in the material realm of culture. Here, too, we encounter the pattern of a decentralized, network-like determination of the relative value of things; here, too, this process is assigned a central ordering function. The political economy of modern times introduces the concept of the market as a replacement for the now "absent ideological centre" of culture (according to Joseph Vogl). The individual members of society, who are no longer coordinated by a faith shared by all, need a new principle of order.

Adam Smith's price theory states that prices are based on supply and demand. Market participants set their prices based on the currently discernible supply of a good or service, and on the presumed preferences and needs of other market participants. If this assessment is successful, the product is sold, if it fails, the unlucky seller is likely to disappear from the market, unless government subsidies are provided. Here we see, as in the case of the modern concept of honor, a process in which the individual, in this case as market participant, can only appraise his own position by actively, and in part speculatively, positioning himself among all everyone else.

Smith did not think of the market price as a completely arbitrary determination. For the market price tended, unless prevented by momentary disruptive factors, towards the "natural price": the price that must be paid for grain, for example, in order to be able to pay wages in the year of harvest, make necessary investments in equipment and seeds, pay any land lease, and feed the farmer. "Profit" is Smith's term for the surplus that has to be made over and above the cost of production in order to be able to do all this and, if necessary, to pay the person(s) involved in planning and controlling production.

The natural price, which Smith also calls the "central price," will, in his view, always prevail on average, over a reasonable period of time. An increase in price beyond that would create incentives for other entrepreneurs to also offer the good in question in order to profit from the increased price, thus increasing the supply and, as a result, lowering the price back towards the natural price. If the "natural price" is undercut, the same mechanism applies, only in reverse; potential suppliers would reduce their production and thus reduce supply, in effect regulating the price upwards.

There is a belief here in the ultimate reasonableness of the results of an uncoordinated process; Smith described it - in a single place, mind you, and rather in passing - as the work of an "invisible hand." We are supposed to have confidence that the results of a self-organizing exchange of goods and services among people will ultimately serve the benefit of all. We are promised that ideologically divided people with different metaphysical beliefs will nevertheless act in accordance with certain principles.

At the same time, Smith says, market participants continually establish a balance that varies within narrow limits, while at the same time improving the welfare of society. Let us concede to Smith that every concrete good has a "real" value and not just a relatively fixed price. (This assumption was plausible for Smith because he was thinking about an economy in narrow spatial confines: transport costs over a radius of several kilometers, for example, were so high that for many goods and services there was in fact a clearly defined local market). The assessment of the others' appreciation of this good motivates the increase or decrease in its price, in relation to the imaginary normal value of the natural price. This guessing game is the economic expression of the typical modern navigation of the individual in the web of the presumed views of others; we see such navigation at work with the modern concept of honor in the external sense of prestige and status.

The analogy to the moral principle of modern times becomes even clearer when we look at the level of currencies. For a currency is a measure by which we fix the price of goods and services. This measure itself has no measure except its relation to other such measures, that is, to other currencies. To ask about the "real value" of a currency is absurd today. After the uncoupling of the currencies of many states to the US dollar, which in turn was secured in gold, it is now nothing but our opinions and our assumptions about the opinions of others that determines the price (relative value) of currencies between themselves. The structures are the same in the moral and material realms of culture; what the market and the associated expectations of order are to the economic realm, the order of prestige is to the social realm.

Not only do we find the described similarity of what happens in the social and economic realms, there is also a similarity in the mistakes typical to both areas shaping our culture. In the economic sphere, there are some who believe in the reasonableness of the results of uncontrolled market activity. In the moral sphere, many of us are convinced that we need only be successful in order to lead a life worth living.

Both are misconceptions: An unregulated market cannot be reasonable. Reason consists precisely in the conscious definition and enforcement of standards for a certain process or type of event. In the same way, a socially successful person does not automatically lead a life of his own in which he finds fulfillment. Success per se does not bring redemption where one is tasked with finding the craft of his own life. And certainly success does not free us from the need to defend our philosophy against the constraints of the order of prestige. On the contrary: If we are successful in the system, the danger increases for us of morally succumbing to the mechanics of business and degenerating into a functionary.

5 Redemption in success?

In the first chapter we formulated the riddle of our normality, before turning in the second chapter to ourselves, the craft of our lives and philosophizing as a natural activity of *all* human beings. In the third chapter, we dealt with the tension inherent in every type of society, between adaptation on the one hand and self-realization on the other; then, prefacing some historical background, we described modern society in general as the order of prestige. This order is determined by the ongoing mutual show of respect between its members, the concrete practicalities of which can vary according to the different situations we encounter. This ritualism of respect, our daily social practice, can be understood as a cult of authority toward the modern sovereign, the human will.

On this basis, we can now reinterpret our present and consider our actual life conditions, which are difficult to recognize on the smooth surfaces of global capitalism. The starting point for this new reflection is my despair at the legacy of industrial society, and the future toward which it seems to lead us and, above all, our children. Lurking in the background is also the troubling question of what role one should play in this society; a question that ultimately everyone has to answer individually for their own lives. We are now talking about the major structures and the 'operating logic' of industrial society. For we are integrated into these structures; they define the developmental framework of our lives.

Let us look ahead to the result which we will approach stepwise: Industrial society separates human existence from reality and disperses it into a mosaic of work environments. Nowhere do we see an image of society in which these 'worlds of work' combine into a coherent whole; that is, unless we invest years of self-reflection and spend extensive time critically reading difficult texts and questioning experienced people. Neither the ability to do this nor the privilege of using one's time in this way, is widespread.

At the same time, our 'world of workplaces' cultivates a pseudo-morality of professional ambition and success in our different work contexts, which can grind down the self-willed, original life of man and slowly transform him into a functionary. To be a functionary means to live spiritually in a constant present tense - in a self-conversation and self-understanding without historical depth and thus also without moral recalcitrance, but with all the more carefree energy for every kind of pursuit. This is the enigmatic state of informed unconsciousness, or perhaps better still, the practical unscrupulousness of our everyday industrial existence. (In the first chapter we also spoke of "moral anesthesia.")

For a functionary has a relationship with the environment and with other people only insofar as they can serve his projects. However, his projects are not really his own, but simply the catalogue of success requirements that he has thoroughly adopted for himself from the institutions of his society. If the carrying out of our lives consists in reflecting on ourselves in light of our experience and thereby in further developing ourselves, then the functionary has died. In his person, man is transformed from a potential critic and reformer of his social order to a simple accomplice of established practice.

Let us now take a closer look at the operating system of industrial society to enter into the exact development of these lines of thought. Our present can be understood as the result of the order of prestige coinciding with the industrialization. More precisely: a race of people that constantly has to cultivate the social status of others and that is thus constantly distracted from itself, coincides with the institutionalized operation of different work environments. From this point of departure, a characteristic social situation and a certain dynamic of events develops, which has spread as far across the world as has European cultural influence.

Distractive stress

We discussed beforehand how the modern age demands that everyone pay homage to others and their projects. This reverence is not limited to speculation about other people's views and their expectations of us, depending on the situation, so that we might practically profit from our insights. Rather, the order of honor cultivates a type of personality whose second nature is to navigate among the real or supposed views of other people. As described in chapter four, this navigational work is the real moral reality of modern times; it reveals a striking parallel and analogy in the market theory of economic life. The expected attitudes and views of others are the fleeting element in which we must orient ourselves: in practical dealings with one other as well as in the marketplace of buyers and sellers.

For us, this means that we are constantly exposed to a draining distraction of our attention from the work on ourselves, from the crafting of our individual life. For in the order of prestige, others immediately curtail their cooperation when they notice that we are not fully prepared to perform the required dance around their presumed expectations and thus guarantee their status. This also has its coherence. For where I do not recognize in someone else respect for my emotions, I have to fear that I will be overlooked or disadvantaged in future decisions made by this person.

That is why paying homage to others in any concrete situation requires our full attention, does not allow for any liberating cynicism or even ironic lightness - small ritual violations suffice to make a mark of respect flimsy and socially worthless. In our society, going from situation to situation means looking at oneself from the outside and asking: "How do I appear to the others at this moment? Does this effect coincide with the presumed expectations that others have of me in this situation? Is there dissonance? If so, what costs might that have for me?"

In large parts of our social life, our minds are fixed not upon ourselves, but upon others, in order to read their expectations of us for the purpose of profiting through conformity or of being able, at least, to keep peace with them. This navigating among the presumed expectations of others, in one situation after another, is constantly, actively self-disconcerting. We are time and again being led away from ourselves, which is why the vast offering of present-day self-help kitsch promises quite plausibly to help us to discover our "true selves", or to assist us on the journey of "coming to ourselves."

The meditation and mindfulness movement is an indication of the constant strain and hectic occupation of our attention, which mature people try to escape - and which many less mature people do not dare to escape, but which they nevertheless want to make bearable. The distraction from ourselves has reached such a degree that it can be declared a "life-changing program" to simply concentrate on our breathing and "be completely present in the moment."

The entertainment industry knows, reinforces and works to ameliorate this stress pattern of our society by presenting it as normal and friendly. The cartoon sagas of the Disney corporation virtually celebrate a cult of the "true self" and the dramatic breakthrough to the "true destiny" of their heroes. Our children's school readings are rife with stories in which individuals assert themselves against the societal pressure to conform, or fail to do so, and essentially become like the criminals they recognize in others. (Think, for example, of William Golding's *Lord of the Flies*, Morton Rhue's *The Wave*, or Max Frisch's *Biedermann and the Arsonists*).

The strong emphasis in different areas of our culture on *finding one's own way* and becoming independent of others, is the product of the existential distraction and dispersion of focus to which we are subject in everyday life. It seems plausible to admonish us to become ourselves, because we are obviously subject to the real danger of spending our lives being something other than ourselves.

Standardized identity: Introducing careers

The advent of industrialization provides outwardly distracted, i.e., uncentered and insecure individuals with a structure of purpose-oriented institutions. This fundamentally changes the cultural situation. The most diverse goals are societally established through their own distinct institutions, each with a special bureaucracy, each with its own strict enforcement of its specific rationality: schools, the military, stock corporations, production plants and service providers of all kinds, administrations, clubs, associations, parties, etc.

These institutions now offer us careers – a well-defined track that we may run for 60 years and more with full-time commitment, a contest to which we are emphatically invited and that is capable of sucking up all our freshness, energy and nerve. A career is the opposite of the path of life that every being charts for itself on the basis of its unique experience - because this path of life is unique and unrepeatable. A career, on the other hand, is something that many need to be able to carry out in roughly the same way; it must be reproducible. In fact, nobody has an 'unprecedented' career because it would then no longer be a career. Unprecedented is only an invention or a pioneering act. "Irreplaceable," according to Jacob Burckhardt, "is only the person endowed with abnormal intellectual or moral power whose actions relate to an ideal" - and that is not the careerist.

After all, to follow a career is to master an obstacle course that in principle anyone can enter. By definition, there is nothing less original than a career. That it is possible to view life from the cradle to the grave as such an obstacle course is significant both for our societal system and for us as individuals.

Those absorbed in advancing their careers do not question the status quo they are faced with. On the contrary, they create demand for more of the known, more of same: for the goods that the system has to offer, that it extolls, and with which it can bind us to itself. For us as individuals, the prospect of being able to look at our whole life as a career represents a certain kind of blessing. For where there is no general consensus on the meaning of this life's pursuit, *business* (busy-ness) is needed. After all, what would we do with ourselves in its absence?

The order of prestige instills in man a sense of insecurity about himself – an existential lack of self-confidence, plunging him into the mental suffering associated with it. The industrial, functionally organized society now creates a biotope for these individuals in the world of work, offering them a simple, relieving deal. We can acquire stability, regularity, direction, rewards, recognition, even a prefabricated whole self, a whole pre-formulated story about ourselves, at the price of eager conformity.

The promise of success in the institution, of a successful career, of advancement, is like a pre-configured self-narrative, a standard identity. Finally, you are *someone*, that is to say: someone with a specific role granted you by other people. And that is much better than being simply disoriented, obviously unoriginal, ordinary like most of us, and what is more alone.

Religion of the functionary

If we are prepared to "make a career," thus accepting and, whether or not wholeheartedly, running through such a standard identity, the labor-intensive and nervous ritualism of respect becomes for us radically defused. For in every institution there are varieties of reputation and status cultivation that are strictly oriented towards the purpose of the institution and that can be learned. Niklas Luhmann has comprehensively analyzed this fact: "All organizations that continuously pursue special purposes form a system of official, formally legitimate expectations (...), a certain basic framework of orientation. (...) In dealings with other members of the organization, everyone can assume that these formal expectations are shared."

Our constitutional ritual of guessing each others' expectations under high uncertainty and social risk, is here replaced with actual knowledge about what others will expect of us. This decreases our risk immensely: For if we know the purpose of the institution and have a basic understanding of its business, we simply know what others expect from us and what they must praise us for if they do not want to "harm the business", i.e. to contradict the purpose of the institution.

This does not mean that human behavior in institutions is then logical within these coordinates, and that this predictability is always really produced us. But our inevitable disputes now have a regulatory framework of 'professionalism.' Within this framework, conflicts can now be talked away, trivialized, dramatized or otherwise opportunistically 'managed' to safeguard the operational requirements of the institution.

The specialized institutions of industrial society relieve our lives of the trauma of metaphysical dislocation and loneliness by offering us special purpose communities with a clear structure and code of conduct. It is only by immersing ourselves in the working world of the institutions that most of us reliably overcome the constant insecurity with which the order of prestige burdens our relationships, and thus our very being. We can now know what is expected of us - what may be considered 'normal' for us.

Indeed, the frequent phrase that something is "quite normal," which we recite to ourselves and others as a consolation in the everyday trials of our industrialized life, has the character of a secular incantation: With this formula we assure ourselves that the cause of our suffering is *legitimate*. "I can't help it," and in the end, I don't have to worry. On the contrary, it is precisely the fact *that* we suffer from the impositions from which people in our institutions normally suffer that becomes the seal of our affiliation. "You had to lay people off. Don't worry, it's normal to lose some sleep over that for a few nights."

In this sense, finding a place in our institutions and taking up the work specific to them creates a sense of security. The acquisition of status becomes an unspectacular matter of calculated exertion. If you want to get an idea of the fascination and deep relief that this insight triggers, it is best to imagine a neat, necktie-clad young professional with shiny shoes.

Our integration into the labor market is the lukewarm redemption from the painful atomization of our families and friends by an industrial society based on the division of labour. This redemption is provided by the system itself, like a peace offer. If we become part of one or more institutions, we experience a firm acceptance into a community that, with a shared goal, is conditionally, but predictably loyal to me. Institutions are therefore the actual temples or churches of the majority faction in our mass societies. They have a pervasive effect on our behavioral motivation because they serve the fundamental human needs of security, regularity and belonging.

Conformity to the standard of an institution makes us all suddenly and undoubtedly *respectable*. We can now expect and award status following clear rules, build up prestige for ourselves, and show respect for others - in other words, cultivate our self-esteem and support that of others at the same time. The need for anxious and nervous self-examination is strongly diminished. The ticket to five-star hotels, airport lounges and business class compartments is not money, it is reliable conformity. As long as we do not appear as people with personal value judgements, but merely as banner bearers of our institution's express purpose, i.e., as functionaries, we need no longer worry about our status.

This was and maybe still is not a given in regard to our friends and relatives, under whose eyes we grew up and spent our 'free time' away from school. Anytime it could have easily happened that someone passed judgement on us in a way that hurt our self-esteem and threw us into doubt. Or we judged ourselves because we felt we were failing. And no one had the power to lift this siege to our soul by others or ourselves; no one could say "it's all right" - because it was really our concern about what would actually be good for us and what kind of person we would subsequently have to become, that made us so vulnerable.

We had to stand up for ourselves, we had to 'grow up' and tell the others: "This is who I am, and this is my point of view." Maybe we even had to insist that "You and your problems are not mine," "I'm going to do this differently," etc. We live in an essentially moral mode in our youth and are fully under the tension between morality and conformity that we have described in the third chapter.

We shape the narrative about ourselves in light of our young experience, for the first time; more or less consciously, we decide what kind of people we want to be and how we want to live. In doing so, we are under the distorting pressure of somehow integrating ourselves professionally for the sake of securing our material livelihood. We have to develop our self-will *in a way that is socially compatible*. It is against the backdrop of our emergence from this moral crisis, which perhaps corresponds to our 'wonderful' youth, that entering the world of work can feel so inspiring, so liberating.

Industrial society is able to channel the energy of our quest for personal identity, for its own purposes; it manages to optimally organize the passionate engagement *especially* of self-insecure persons for any purpose. Companies and public administrations are particularly fond of hiring "insecure overachievers" – people who strive for high achievement out of a feeling of self-doubt and apprehensiveness. The institutions of industrial society accomplish the psychological feat of providing people *through their work* with a sense of real satisfaction that stems from professionalism and success.

Professionalism stands for correct thinking and doing in terms of any given operation's purpose, which is experienced as the fulfillment of moral requirements. Success stands for the yield of laborious professionalism, which is experienced as the reward for moral virtue. Professionalism and success can make people immensely satisfied and give them a sense of righteousness, although neither has anything to do with morality or virtue. One who fulfills the purpose assigned to him by his institution, does not in any sense express reservations about what is going on about him, as would independent reflection. He therefore shows no moral virtue, but its exact opposite, conformity. That is why I speak of the *pseudo-moral* satisfaction of professionalism and success - and later of the *pseudo-moral* madness of ambition, that is, of deliberate and zealous conformity.

With its offer of institutional security and the drug of success, industrial society easily secures the loyalty of many, even a quasi-religious devotion to the operations of their institution. Young management consultants, "trainees" and apprentices with their closely interlocked "studies" of boring standard business or legal recipes for desired practical results, with their eternal marathon of internships and their uniform-like corporate suits, show no less piety in their industrial ambition than the most submissive monastic student may show piety in the Christian faith.

For the functionary, professional practice is the *religio*, the reassurance of what is decisive for his existence in his daily thoughts and actions. This explains the unlimited fanaticism with which modern institutions have been and are being served; they, not the established religions, deliver most of us from our painful lack of belonging, insecurity and insignificance that comes with the liberation of man out of the bonds of religious tradition. This is why in recent history, perfectly normal workers and consumers of every hue – given appropriate superiors – could so often and so smoothly turn into perfectly normal criminals.

Without resolute intellectual resistance based on one's own value judgments, immersing oneself in this game of careerism can cast a spell over the entire existence of the individual, transforming him from a unique human being into a replaceable functionary. If this sounds too dramatic, consider for a moment the cases you know in which a person's 'work life' has ruined his family life and other personal relationships.

Let us hope that no reader of this book recognizes himself as such a case: moral emptiness, a complete lack of deeper human relationships or coldness in his personal dealings with the few associates that remain, accompanied by a senseless excess of material goods and their unbridled 'enjoyment'; intellectual stupefaction in the midst of a storm of chatter, actionism and intricate habits of consumption bordering on the ridiculous.

It is common to speak of "inhumane" behavior, for example, in the case of acts of war or other crimes, but certainly also in the case of small everyday behaviors that betray the malicious moral bankruptcy of a person. So our language knows that people can act as non-humans, as *something else*; this dehumanized alternative of how our bodies and minds can be in the world *without* being human is existence as a functionary. Professional work and success according to the pattern of the institutions of industrial society is the religion of functionaries, their ambition is their piety.

The Myth of success

So how does this thing called 'career' proceed with us? What does it do to us to let us operate reliably in the manner requested of us, draining our moral energy in the process? There is no typical biographical starting point for this exploration, but the institutions of our society lead us toward taking a 'career path' early on by teaching us its form and logic. We accustom our children to daycare before they start their school careers, where each institution prepares them specifically for the demands of the next. Norbert Elias has noted that the amount of time spent in such educational institutions has steadily increased in modern times, in line with the growing disciplinary demands of society on its members.

At every point along the way it is claimed that our integration in this very institution serves to prepare us for 'life' or 'reality.' "It is not for school, it is for life that we learn." (Lucius Annaeus Seneca) – this is an honest expression of the fact that our schooling is not really 'life'. Our school career consists of a sequence of games with strict rules, which are designed to introduce us to the standards of life to open us up to the seriousness of things before we are allowed to experience them ourselves and recreate them for the next generation.

We are being prepared to take on a clearly defined function. This education teaches discipline, i.e., the ability to restrict and concentrate one's gaze, feeling, thinking, and doing. People look for a path of life that suits them personally and specifically, institutions offer standardized careers; the unnatural effort to bridge this contradiction is called "training." At the end of this process, we need to have developed discipline - if we do not want to literally fall outside the framework of society.

Then we enter our "work life," our "professional life," the "world of work" - all expressions that suggest a comprehensive ordering of our time and an all-pervading sense of meaning and direction for our future. For all these expressions have a logical peculiarity in common: they combine a term which refers to an aspect of life - "work," "profession" - with the more or, arguably, the most general concept of all: "life." This makes "work life," "professional life," and "world of work" terms that are self-contradictory, since they suggest a placing of the whole (life) at the service of a certain partial process of life (work, profession). In German, this is particularly conspicuous because the concepts are expressable in one word: *Arbeitsleben* (work life), *Berufsleben* (professional life), *Arbeitswelt* (world of work).

Viewed in this way, these terms have a clear ideological thrust: they suggest the norm that the sub-process of work is at the center of life, identifiable even with life as a whole. After all, the most "productive" and docile "human capital" is the human being who directs everything in his life towards work.

Were one to seek a few unspectacular, less general examples for this approach, the absurdity of word creations like "professional life" and "world of work" really comes to the fore. Seen logically, it is as though one would want to enjoy one's snack time at his piece of table-furniture or play some tennis-sport. The point to notice is that a concept with a narrower scope of meaning (like 'work') is erroneously treated on a par with a concept massively larger scope of meaning (like 'life').

As soon as the transition from the … well, probably from our *past* life into our work life has been successful, a certain dynamic sets in; a certain program runs its course with us. This program is able to turn our place of work into what even reasonable people often refer to as "their world." And it is true: Each of the special-purpose communities in which we pursue our careers can be experienced from the inside as a world of its own, however narrowly limited the meaning and purpose of each of these institutions may be. (And the meaning of each institution *is* limited. Limitation of meaning is the essence of every institution; it is legitimized solely by the very purpose it serves.)

Industrial society needs and cultivates the concept 'success' as psychological fuel, as a compensatory moment for monotony and lack of meaning. Success serves in the system as a drug and manipulative instrument; success divides our often highly meaning-deprived work into phases of concentrated exertion and then consumption of the carrot we have won, thus making it bearable. In the pursuit of success, we are effecting our ever-closer entanglement with the ongoing operations of our particular industrial business

To recognize this, one must first break with the habit of thinking that success in itself is meaningful and valuable. This prejudice is hard to overcome; after all, who would want to be unsuccessful? However, we are successful or unsuccessful only in terms of the exact requirements that we or others set for us. These demands are based on value concepts that are not without alternative even where they seem to us self-evident. They always have to be explained, as, of course, one does not want to be subject to them unwittingly and possibly, with one's whole personal existence, fall victim to them.

The price of a naive "hurray" attitude to success is high, the danger to our prospects of fulfillment in life is great. Success is a treacherous construct that we must be wary of. Speaking of a "success" means declaring a certain result to be meaningful and desirable; it *does not* mean naming a fact. Success is organized, and it does not represent a harmless contrivance but the erection of a dubious idol, a veritable fortress in which our thoughts and feelings can be fixated.

First of all, success does not seem to be for ordinary people with ordinary abilities. Rather, when we talk about success, we think of talented, powerful, fanatically diligent people; but in any case, we think of people who are in some way capable of distinguishing themselves before others. Figuratively, we imagine successful people favorably illuminated and with a clear profile before a blurry but deep and wide background. Success is special and must therefore be the exception.

A culture that concentrates on that special thing, on the exceptional case of success, and makes it the object of veneration and therefore of ambition, will constantly send a depressing message: Everything ordinary, quotidian, boring about us must be due to our lack of success, our failure. This is a psychologically torturous idea, which engenders feelings of inferiority and thus fuels the struggle to escape the 'loser' existence of bland normality through success. Marketing people know exactly what they are doing when they fill their advertising cosmos with invitations to the consumer to recognize his "uniqueness,", to "activate" and to "live" it, and with many other idiotic, but smartly selected phrases.

Someone may be considered a successful businessman if he doubles his capital within a year. Is this achievement significant and valuable? Maybe he had 50 million before this year and now he has 100, but his family was ruined during that year by his constant absence, exhaustion and depression. Was it a successful year? Or let's look at another example from "investment banking," which grabbed so much headline attention. This is a field that is far too little understood, and whose players, not least because of this, get away with unbelievable crimes against the common good all over the world.

Employees of an "investment bank" are in fact gamblers in a casino: They speculate on the performance of shares or debt securities and issue certificates by means of which bets can be placed on such developments. Such a gambler ("investment banker") thus acquires the purchase rights to large parts of the next corn harvest, say in Peru, through various letterbox companies belonging to his casino, i.e. the company employing him we mislabel "bank". Now he sells a piece of paper to wealthy private individuals with the following content: "You may buy from me at time X so and so many tons of corn at the guaranteed price P. But you don't have to do that, it's only an *option*. To attain this option, you pay me a small fee today."

Now the buyers of these certificates wait until time X and watch how the corn price in Peru develops. If the corn price at time X is *above* the agreed fixed price P, they use their certificate and buy corn, which they then resell for the higher market price and therefore at a profit. The casino operators ("investment bankers") had, of course, already made money with the fees for these certificates; now, in a second step, they sit on the corn harvest they managed to obtain, until the price rises to the desired level. Then they themselves move to sell and cash in once more. The poor people of Peru pay 25% more per package of cornmeal bread directly to the rich private individuals holding the said certificates and to the casino, whose lead gambler receives a huge bonus. Was this a success for the owner of the certificates and the "investment banker"?

In both cases, the answer can only be "yes" if you consider money-grubbing to be the highest value, the guiding norm of life, and if you consider people's well-being to be less important than your own financial gain. That is, the answer is "yes" if you are one of those people, as Spinoza describes them, "of impotent mind, whose greatest happiness is to look at the money in the box and cram their belly." (This type of character is particularly common in countries where public goods such as health, water, land, education and training, etc. are at the mercy of the market. Because there, as a private person, one has to buy them at maximum prices and is thus forced to horde money if one does not want to live miserably).

Success and life satisfaction do not necessarily coincide. People can be very successful by different standards without being satisfied with their lives and themselves. Satisfaction depends on what goals we set for ourselves and how we treat ourselves and others in pursuit of them. The philosophy of the Stoics says in effect, 'If we focus on purposes that are inherently uncertain and fickle (such as wealth, fame, or sensual pleasure), we must be prepared for a constant up and down, perhaps with some stretches of euphoria and certainly with regular frustrations.' On this path, we also constantly invite the suffering that comes with comparing ourselves with others. We can successfully devote ourselves to these traditional goals and become completely unhappy, even to the point of committing suicide.

The myth that success is simply *the* key to fulfillment is useful toward mobilizing us for the operational purposes of our institutions. Our prejudice that success in *itself* is important and valuable motivates us in the right direction for the industrial system. Thus, in the operation of industrial society, success and recognition are awarded to an individual exactly to the extent that he devotes himself or herself solely to the purpose of the institution. This can mean making money or fulfilling a certain administrative function.

The moment we consider our moral autonomy and ask whether the success to be achieved in our working world is actually desirable, we go missing to the system as functionaries. Ideas of a social good superordinate to the company, of an overarching meaning, are just as irrelevant to the securing of trophies of success as is the telling of a comprehensive story of oneself. On the contrary: success bonuses are awarded to those who are particularly skillful in helping to *outplay* public interest and the common good in favor of the narrow goals of a certain institution. Success is achieved by those who put aside reflecting about themselves in the light of their experience, and who narrow their thinking and actions to functioning in the work context, i.e., who 'optimize' themselves. Careerists think within strict limitations in a deliberate and disciplined way, anticipating to the best of their ability what will most likely be expected of them in each consecutive situation.

The Dignity of profit

Our various work spheres can be conceived as institutions of salvation: They organize for their functionaries opportunities to have success. Organized success is offered to us as glue for our fragmented identity. The struggle for success in our careers is the usual way in which we learn to strive for self-assurance and fulfillment. Our life then gains structure and direction *not* from pursuing self-designed goals, but from adapting to the expectations that superiors, colleagues, customers, 'stakeholders' or simply 'society' presumably have of us.

Industrial society is suited perfectly to turn its members away from themselves, and instead focus their attention fully on the institutions they contribute to. This reflects the fact that we, as inhabitants of the order of prestige, are systematically and constantly made insecure of ourselves. Our constant effort to navigate the expectations that we assume others have of us, depending on the situation, is *practiced* self-insecurity: How do I have to be in this particular moment in order to find acceptance?

If success is the modern promise of salvation, then this promise costs us dearly; it is "not salvation from evil, but evil salvation" (Thomas Mann). First of all, its basic rationale, one excuses the drastic expression, is *idiotic*: we strive for self-confidence in the struggle for success by pursuing self-uncertainty with the sporting zeal of our ambition. After all, the ongoing adaptation to the changing expectations of changing groups of people in our careers requires a continual, almost consciously fostered uncertainty about our effect on others.

You might as well seek inner peace in a nightclub or concentration at a fair. We strive for personal fulfillment in the fight for success. But this struggle forces us to avoid conceiving *our own* wishes and goals, which we could then fulfill *in our own way.* Our striving for personal fulfillment becomes a perverted instrument for the fulfillment of capital interests. And this idiocy is contagious: "No one errs for himself alone, but he is always the cause of the error of others" (Lucius Annaeus Seneca).

Moreover, the industrialization of man into a functionary who has to earn his living (who therefore, as is implied by the salient expression "O earn a living", does not *simply and self-evidently* deserve to live), means that every inalienable aspect, every undisputed intrinsic value is denied the individual. The value of the functionary is determined solely by his clearly defined usefulness as a supplier of labour and is ultimately a monetary value. There is the further function of the concept of 'success', and the practice of making functionaries successful, in which every institution engages: The tool 'succcss' is also necessary because the value of a person is considered unproven in industrial society before he creates benefit, i.e., monetary value for his institution. Success is the authentication of our monetary value, the proof that our life has earned its keep and is not 'parasitic.'

Anyone who industrializes himself for the sake of his career is therefore not only behaving idiotically in practice, but is also forsaking his dignity.

According to Kant's ingenious insight, dignity belongs to that which has no price, but which determines the price of all other things *as its standard*. In industrial society, money in the form of profit is imbued with dignity, but not only *money*, because money, like machines, land, real estate and everything else, is only a form of capital (Karl Marx would say: a commodity). What matters for the industrial dignity of money is that something more is made of the capital than was initially invested. Industrial dignity rests on *profit*. Whoever wants to exist in industrial society, must sell his work as a commodity and thus feed it into the 'circulation process,' into the 'turnover' (Karl Marx) of capital; in turn, he can only continue and at least temporarily secure his livelihood if he continuously turns a profit.

According to the logic of capitalism, profit thus serves as the yardstick that *de facto* determines the price of all other things: The expectation of profit determines the price of labour, the rights granted to the worker to enjoy rest, health, care, etc., the willingness to invest in a certain country, the amount of bribes ('donations') to political parties, etc. Thus, profit is established as the guiding value, the only value in itself. The idea of profit itself is removed from criticism and evaluation, it rules absolutely, unless a compensating welfare state secures some public goods from it through solidarity financing.

The circus of success and failure is an absolute necessity for the industrial system because profit - and not man with his needs and rights - is regarded as decisive and inviolable in this system. The human being, thus *institutionally* degraded, is actually of no decisive significance in a world that seems only to consist of interlocking working worlds and nature as their raw material reservoir. In order to alleviate this nightmare, he must be shown a way to secure for himself in relation to the institution a right to respect and thus a right to a livelihood. We understand our degradation and accordingly we fight vehemently for success and for the status symbols that authenticate it, tormented by fears of failure.

The pseudo-moral façade

In the struggle for our right to exist in industrial society, we move within a finely balanced framework. The function-oriented institutions build a moral façade that is intended to make our exclusively purpose-driven actions morally as comfortable and painless as possible. In front of this façade, those who play their part can experience a deep pseudo-moral satisfaction that potentially permeates the whole of everyday life. The best term to describe this pseudo-morality of our institutions is 'professionalism.'

Internally, each institution has its own set of rules, hierarchy and, in the behavior of its members, a certain cultural coherence. Compliance with the rules of the organization is praised and rewarded, just as is a pragmatic approach taken to all other factors that may come into play and might have a bearing on the fulfillment of institution goals, such as state laws and moral obligations. In many large companies, e.g., entire departments 'optimize,' i.e., minimize the taxes to be paid to stated, and 'enlighten' political actors in matters pertaining to the interest of company profit.

The outward forms of general morality - praise and blame, public recognition of special achievements, etc. – have their analogues in function-oriented organizations: declarations of company values, behavioral guidelines, kitschy talk about the employee's loyalty and personal commitment to his tasks at anniversaries, pins, 'thank you' and award ceremonies, and rankings of the best salespeople, project managers or the most effective executives. The internal propaganda of the institutions cultivates the appropriate rhetoric for this purpose, which is never ashamed to cite moral vocabulary.

There is also the talk of "passion" for and "devotion" to the job. And in "interviews" and "features," laboratory technicians, accountants and CEOs employ the same phrases to present themselves as noble souls who "make a difference in the world" and "seek to improve the lives of those we serve." (Siegfried Kracauer quotes in his classic *Die Angestellten* (*The Employees*) from a company newspaper that spreads this kind of pseudo-moral propaganda. He recounts that critical workers christened the publication "The Slime Trumpet.")

All of this, taken together, can lead to a veritable illusion of moral unity and moral integrity of an industrial enterprise, promoting a quasi-religious devotion to it. Successful action replaces moral action in the institutions, but is treated as moral probation in its external forms and rituals. One pretends that the enterprise is a moral institution. All this is kitsch - it aims high and hits low. (This beautiful definition stems from a journalist whose name I have forgotten). But it actually satisfies many people whose entire practical energy is focused on their work.

The lifelong pursuit of hierarchical advancement and rank promotion cannot simply be explained by the fact that people are offered more money. Money comes as part of a package of symbols of success and thus social status, which are in reality only symbols of servility to the institution. This is not disguised at all within the system: Employees are one resource among others in the production process, they are 'human resources.' This is why the departments that deal with personnel matters are often called "Human Resources."

This mentality promotes the complete loss of moral or political reflection in our institutions. In the resulting vernacular, liars, slanderers and manipulators become "difficult," "energetic" or "opinionated" colleagues. Established corruption becomes a "challenge in customer management." And in fact, it is of no use at all for the declared business purpose of an institution to express moral judgments. It does, however, sometimes benefit the operating result to ignore the moral reality of a given predicament and ask which vocabulary can best help to harness the energy of the situation for the operative purpose.

The "opinionated" colleague is then specifically asked at the beginning of the meeting for his assessment, and this - whatever it may be - is then scanned for useful elements by the superior, praised to the skies, and repeatedly taken up in a moderating manner during the discussion. The troublemaker is thus hugged to death. The corrupt marketing manager is transferred to a position "where his talents can flourish even better," unless he "decides to take advantage of development opportunities outside the company." Inconvenient senior civil servants or military personnel are sent into temporary retirement.

The prostitution of all gestures and practices of morality and reason to the merely purpose-driven enterprise is a decisive cultural resource of industrial society. Like everything else, people are regarded as things that can be used rationally. Therefore, everything that seems important and worthwhile to people is a potential means of motivation for the institution. As motivation for success, our needs, hopes and inclinations are built into the prison walls of our work environments.

In our workplaces, we are exposed to a whole system of influence and control that must not be confused with reality. In our institutions, we work in a culture of manipulative relativism. Whatever the employee qua "human resource" needs in order to function, is granted to him: What he needs to hear, is said, what he presumably does not want to hear, is, as far as possible, excluded from discussion, what he believes to be true, is confirmed, what he condemns, is duly scolded, if possible. Only his critical questions or feelings of disdain regarding the meaning and global consequences of his industrial work, are certainly nowhere to be found. After all, it would be quite unprofessional to 'philosophize' in this way.

6 How the 'world of work' replaces reality

The seemingly unreal cruelties selectively reported in our evening news and the social and technical achievements of industrial societies have something in common: they emerge as co-productions of different work environments – of different 'worlds of work.' (For lack of a better English term, we will continue to use *world(s) of work* for the German *Arbeitswelt*; this is a term which, taken literally, seems to invest professional labor with a magical power to constitute a coherent universe for one engaged in its.

In these separate spheres of rational exertion, ambitious people pursue their success. In doing so, they can feel like complete human beings morally anchored in a community, even though that is far from the truth. In fact, our work environment obstructs our view of reality by placing us firmly in a space of self-contained rationality. Nothing in our work life is as it appears from the perspective of our everyday experience. We now have to describe a wide arc of reflection and argumentation in order to gain clarity about the actual relationship of our work environments to reality.

First we inquire into the notion of a *world of work* in greater detail, then we distinguish it precisely, i.e., meticulously and with no tolerance for ambiguities, from reality. For it is our intellectually careless handling of these terms that is part of the actuarial reserve on which industrial society relies to secure our loyalty. These considerations then give us an opportunity to reflect even more closely on rationality and reason, and, particularly, to ask how exactly they actually differ from one another.

The fact that rationality and reason are not the same thing has been already mentioned here and there before, but the distinction must be formulated more precisely. A closer examination of their difference reveals that our concern for reality - that is, for the actual well-being of ourselves, others and the world - is expressed only in *reasonable* thought. *Rational* thought, on the other hand, indicates in a very specific sense only the deliberate, possibly unconscionable turning away from reality. In this sense, one can also define the terms "realism" and "pragmatism" that often appear in politics and elsewhere: Realism is the attitude in which we want to approach reality reasonably and improve it. Pragmatism, on the other hand, is the management of existing purposes and their respective rationality at the expense of reality.

A world of work?

Let us begin with a distinction between idea and concept of experience, loosely based on Kant's *Critique of Pure Reason*. It is helpful in analyzing and correctly classifying the strange term *world of work*. Concepts of experience can be understood on the basis of our perceptions, in one way or another, and they can be clarified by means of examples; we can show each other what a table and what a chair is, and then we understand it immediately. For an idea, however, in Kant's vernacular, "no congruent (i.e., corresponding; note Andrick) object can be given in the senses." An idea as a "pure concept of reason" cannot be illustrated empirically.

Karl Hepfer suggests a brilliant illustration of the essence of Kant's idea: Imagine a complex, colorful wall painting in a Renaissance palace. What looks upon entering the hall like a wild jumble of people, horses, weapons, houses and trees, blends into a harmonious whole from exactly one point of view; this is the place in the hall from which we look at the elements of the painting from their common vanishing point. This vanishing point is not to be found on the painting's surface; it is located in the depth of space behind and outside the painting. And yet we can only recognize the meaning and the peculiar beauty of the work of art we are beholding by aligning our perspective with this point. This point is the idea, the unifying aspect of the matter.

In addition to "freedom" and "immortality," Kant considers the idea of the "world" to be philosophically indispensable. "World" refers to the ultimate connectedness of all possible experience in a whole; this whole is what we call reality. In principle, the idea of reality helps us to cope with our concrete experiences. In its light, we consider our experiences as belonging to an overall context, one that our current knowledge and life experience have already to a certain extent opened up to us. The idea of reality thus has the same function for the social sphere as has our idea of the human self for each one of us. The idea of reality assures us that our plans and efforts are ultimately at home in a comprehensive context of regular connections.

Even if we do not know this ultimate comprehensive context (and in Kant's view, we cannot ever recognize it), we can at least surmise it by considering the regularity and predictability of large parts of our experience. The idea of the self, to which the second chapter was devoted, means the bringing together of our different experiences in a narrative of ourselves that gives meaning, direction and unity to our lives. Such a narrative of ourselves needs a stable, predictable framework, and the idea of reality provides this. Viewed as a whole, our language embodies this idea and brings order to our relationship with things and other people.

In a certain sense we are overwhelmed by the ideas of "self" and "world": Our experience is limited, our memory is dim and sketchy, our intellect is flawed. We are also bound to a unique experiential standpoint, which we cannot transcend. Therefore we can never fully grasp and express the totality toward which the ideas of reality and the self are directed. Everyone has only a small part of all possible experience; everyone remains enigmatic even to himself to a certain extent. We cannot completely escape our preconscious imprints and thought patterns, nor can we fully understand what exactly new experiences will trigger in us.

Nevertheless, the idea of a general whole (i.e., of reality) and the idea of an individual whole (i.e., of the self) provides us with a framework in which our experience can find context and our life can acquire direction and meaning. Only in the awareness of being in reality as a self can we *actually live*; for life is the work on ourselves in the light of our experience. And this work is only possible if we can rely on an order of the whole that makes our experience regular and thereby our behavior predictable. 'Reality' and 'self' are the names of two principles of unity, of cohesion, by means of which we create and retain in reflection the meaning of all things and of our individual lives.

The concept of a 'world of work' (*Arbeitswelt*) is therefore an irredeemably inconsistent notion from the outset, as we have already discussed briefly in the previous chapter. The factual situation implied in it - a world that *consists of work* in one sense or another - is impossible: 'world' stands for reality, the overall context of things; the term 'world of work' refers to this world, but with the absurd implication that the world thus designated comprises only one part of the world, viz. work. This is a contradiction in terms.

Therefore, the 'world' to which the expression 'world of work' refers cannot be reality. Nevertheless, the tendency to speak of the strictly limited sphere of, say, a certain professional environment as if it were reality, is understandable. In a simple, undeniable sense, we live in a world that — wherever it is not brute nature, but cultivated - can be viewed as a mosaic of worlds of work.

In the business world there is talk of the "world of research," the "world of marketing," etc. Every banal thing seems to have its own 'world': "motor world," "soccer world," "cosmetics world"; in Germany, there are also politically more modest coinages like 'Kaufland' (literally: 'Shopping Country') or Volkswagen's 'Autostadt' ('car city'). From the same mentality that produces such expressions, we speak of 'work life' and the 'world of work.'

And these supposedly distinct 'worlds' are then addressed by the guardians of operational rationality, with the concept of 'work/life balance,' putting work in logical opposition to an individual's life as if it were an alien domain. This brutally honest concept shows that work, charged with total, 'world-creating' meaning, is in fact something from which human life must be protected as from a threatening counter-power.

Every institution, every establishment of our industrial society is a 'world of work' that would like to present itself *pars pro toto as* the whole world, for the purpose of ensuring our unwavering commitment to its purpose. A part presents itself as the whole, at our expense. And this deception often succeeds because our work routine literally trains us to accept this error. The many years of our career occupy our memory and determine our sense of normality. And they offer us that inner-worldly salvation through professionalism and success of which we spoke in the previous chapter.

The path to a world of 'worlds'

This culture and social order of 'worlds of work' did not come into being by historical happenstance. It is logically related to the order of prestige, which evolved as it was met by the unfolding of industrialization and other factors. We now have to explain this compelling connection in order to see even more precisely the situation in which we actually find ourselves in managing our lives today.

Man had to subject the world to his will when God's will no longer seemed clearly recognizable. The Christian life, in which everyone was situated in his legitimate station, now became the Christian religion of different confessions (denominations). Disputes cannot be settled in a binding manner by referring to the views of my confession or to its ministers, if my counterpart adheres to a different confession. Thus our will (instead of the alleged will of God) became ruler, sovereign of the world. The result is the order of prestige. It requires us to play the game of mutual respect, teaching us to carefully consider our effect on others, depending on the situation we find ourselves in at any given point, and to control that effect as far as possible.

This revolution, in which people subjected themselves to the will of their peers and thus raised each other to the rank of equality, continued to bring about the Enlightenment movement. Its representatives demanded reasonable justification of our social institutions, and they also offered such reasonable justifications of varying depth and clarity. The order of prestige is the social implementation of the enthronement of the human will as ruler of the world; the Enlightenment is then the official proclamation of a new right: everything that now seeks to claim validity is to be subjected to the judgment of human reason. Whatever claims to power and obedience that, based on the accustomed und relatively unified corporative ideology of the Middle Ages, still seemed to assert themselves into the bright new age of reason, were subjected to severe criticism.

According to the Enlightenment, that which claims validity should "have authority based on reasons" (Georg F. W. Hegel); man should dare to "use his own intellect," overcome his "self-inflicted immaturity," no longer fear "shadows," and develop a "reasonable estimation of the living forces" (Immanuel Kant). This is an empowerment project in favor of reason and at the same time a disciplinary program for the new sovereign of the world, the human will.

This project demanded analysis: the dissection of traditional institutions, authorities, morality and religiosity into what was considered to be their components, their driving principles. New academic disciplines with freshly delineated subject areas are a testimony to the results of these efforts. At the same time, a diverse literature and art is developing, which often focuses on the plight of the overburdened individual who is now responsible for the ordering of the world, and who suffers from this fate. A completely new cultural landscape emerged that laid the foundation for our world divided into 'worlds of work,' and at the same time sought to overcome those intellectually and emotionally.

Everything must be able to *justify* itself in this new culture - be it a social institution, a law, a custom, or a particular action. Each individual thing must therefore be able to demonstrate a *rationality*, an explanation of its purpose and a statement of its functionality. The iconoclasm of the Reformation and Enlightenment is followed by stocktaking: without a generally shared, meaningful overall picture of the world and of man's role in it, we are only left with the practice of justifying clearly defined purposes to establish order.

The regular (i.e., institutional) fulfillment of these very specific purposes benefits our society in a precisely defined way, and *only* this justifies the authority granted to the acting persons and their organizations. This is the deeper, both historical and logical reason for the emergence of the modern institutions in whose 'worlds of work' we find ourselves.

Our essential mental ability and habit, almost the standard operation of our thinking, has therefore become asking about the purpose and functioning of the things or circumstances we encounter. It always seems most immediately informative to inquire about the purpose of an action, an institution, even a remark or question. Also, at the beginning of a new acquaintance, we are most likely to talk about the profession, the function of a person.

This general line of inquiry also immediately captivates the results of our reflection and artistic articulation. We ask what art and philosophy are actually good for, and so we do not notice that without art and philosophy, we would not even know what it is that may make one thing good and the other bad for us. Works of art and philosophical reflection alone lead us beyond the given and the customary and enable us to long for and pursue what might be better and more beautiful. In the everyday life of our industrialized world, however, the question of what course of action, what belief or principle has the best reasons supporting it, is neglected in favor of the question of which actions, beliefs or principles are factually supported by already *established, accepted, socially powerful* reasons.

Thinking that is purpose-driven, which is indispensable for the post-Enlightenment era, always carries with it the danger of cutting off the critical and creative potential of reflection, and of turning us into well-trained idiots - people who cannot get out of their habitual perspective on themselves and the world because they have not learned, or have forgotten, how to ask critical questions. The minuscule numbers of humanities students in the heavily industrialized countries are evidence of this disinterest in questioning the given, and of the general eagerness to join in whatever game is being played.

The most important question that is put to us as idiots-in-the-making is that of the function that we ourselves intend one day to fulfill. In the words of Friedrich Nietzsche, who described the German education system in the late 19th century: "Everywhere there is an indecent haste, as if something were lost if a young man at the age of 23 is not yet *ready*, i.e., not yet able to answer the *main question*: which profession?"

We are trained from an early age to become explorers of 'worlds of work,' and we grow up with the basic understanding that we will one day have to settle into one of them - in order to draw nothing less from it than our "livelihood." This expression makes it clear that we are dealing with the most serious of all demands made upon us. In a functionally divided society, we can devote our entire lifetime to integrating ourselves into one 'world of work' after another, with each one's respective rationality. Someone switches from one function to another, and says: "I'm going to do something else now." But in reality, he simply does the same thing in another direction; he plays out the patterns of rational thought and action according to another guiding purpose.

Using a clarifying exaggeration, we may view our life as a career that traverses one narrowly concentrated, monomaniacal 'world of work' after the other. Each one has a natural tendency to infuse our entire existence with boredom. On the one hand, we are petitioners in our institutions; we seek them out in order to use them for the sole thing of which they are capable and for whose sake they exist. We enter their buildings expecting only one thing; we therefore find ourselves bored and in a mode of passive suffering. And we encounter people there who have only one thing to do, who are dedicated to only one business, who are therefore professional, and who therefore are just as bored and in the same mode of silent suffering.

On the other hand, we ourselves are functionaries in one or more of these institutions, and provide their customers or applicants with the service for which we are employed there. From the attitude with which employees meet us at their place of work, we can see how they have coped with the lack of meaning in their everyday activities. What is normal here is made clear by the fact that the vast majority of job advertisements explicitly call for 'commitment' or 'engagement,' i.e., for unsolicited personal initiative. Obviously, nobody can reasonably assume that the fascination of the job would in and of itself encourage a 'proactive' attitude.

Displacement of the real

What is fundamental cannot be obvious; we do not notice it, but rather simply suffer from it: *specialization* is a basic coordinate of our industrial existence and a danger to our vitality. Our constant adaptations to the 'world of work,' our passage through various institutions, and the compensatory exercises that we may undertake along the way, do not naturally add up to a human life for us. We overwork ourselves, we are 'stressed out,' and then reward ourselves with cigarettes, consumer goods, avowedly purpose-free (and thus subtly stressful) periods of vacation, with gluttony and sex.

This is a reaction to our everyday industrial life, which expects every day something very specific from each functional role, but this from nobody specific, and that means *not really from us*: everyone is replaceable. We all exist to a certain extent in a cycle of blunting through limited work and momentary consolation, which allows us to carry on and, not infrequently, to simply direct our hopes toward the next break.

But to live means to work on oneself in the light of one's experience. Life requires reflection. However, spending our time in constant adaptation, we get by with simple thinking and simple doing. We are offered norms of behavior and routines to follow, that correspond to the purpose of the institution in which we find ourselves. We can function and do not have to reflect and act as moral persons, we can 'just do.' In other words, we can *work rationally* and do not have to *act reasonably*.

This is the dynamic of our present; it leads us away from building and caring for ourselves, from thoughtfully processing our experience, and from continually retelling our personal story. Realism, understood as a conscious reference to reality, is not required of us; reason, that is, the thorough classification and evaluation of our experiences and the conscious design of a good future, is not required. It suffices for our success to behave *rationally* from day to day in the sense of the given purposes.

According to the Enlightenment's, reason, on the other hand, is concerned with the improvement of man and of life with the guiding idea of the public good. As the order of prestige is confronted with industrialization, this conception of enlightening reason is challenged by a web of different rationalities; this is the process of the functional differentiation of society that characterizes modernity: Every institution of our society has its own rationality, its own particular and specific expediency.

The optimized exercise of this rationality in our institutions displaces considerations among its staff and managers as to what would serve human beings in general (and not merely the purpose of the institution). Comprehensive thinking based on the whole of reality is excluded in every sphere of rationality, in every 'world of work.' - Hence it appears *as its own world*; but it is at best a partial world, not reality.

The "morality" of success and the "reason" of professionalism in a 'world of work' are therefore a pseudo-morality and a pseudo-reason. Whoever ventures beyond the institutionally organized ritualism of success and professionalism and asks about reality, that is, whoever inquires about the interconnection of one's own purpose with all others and about the result of this complex, leaves the consensus space of discussion.

The question of reality is something exotic when taken up within an institution; and raising it must be understood as a kind of provocative joke. Whoever insists on it, will sooner or later be shown the door. Moral action that even modestly defers the purpose of the institution or even subordinates it to its own values is 'unprofessional.' One is always just one question away from encountering the ruling principle. I, too, have almost never insisted while at work ...

In this sense, industrial society separates us from reality and rewards our turning away from it. The almost complete absorption of our activities and our thinking in work environments causes reality to disappear. We spoke earlier of the two intellectual 'brackets' with which, in life, we can create and retain meaning for ourselves - the ideas of reality and the self. The first bracket is thus removed by industrial society: because reality is nowhere an issue and is 'irrelevant' and 'extraneous' to every institution; wanting to reflect on its operational purpose in the overall context of reality, is 'unprofessional.'

But the second bracket, that of the self, can never be completely undone. Therein lies the prospect of being able to remain a human being in industrial society. Individually and in small groups, reflection is always possible. But the act of narrating to ourselves what our experience means for our past and for our path into the future, is complicated by a constant distraction that is caused by the social requirement of guessing at the plausible expectations held by others in our social relationships. The pressure to professionalize, which goes hand in hand with the global distribution and networking of value creation and thus competition, further intensifies this problem.

Rationality and reason

Let us continue to explore the difference between rationality and reason; then the full extent of the distance from reality that our institutionalized life entails will become clear. Rationality and reason are not static, rigid structures or merely abstract concepts. They are possibilities of the mind, i.e., something that we can intellectually 'organize' by deliberately handling our attention. Rational and reasonable behavior follow, respectively, a very specific ethos.

Rationality is the obedient pursuit of given purposes, which promises us success. Reason is the conscious selection *and* pursuit of purposes that we consider to be the right ones. Reasonable action, therefore, does not promise success, but conflict. For it signifies my – at least momentary - departure from the given structures; a break in the loyalty to the institutions of which I am a part, and possibly even a break in the loyalty to my social group. Those who are reasonable have reflected and will therefore be able to express what it is they wish to stand up for. Those who behave simply rationally never need to ask this question.

Rationality is the most sparing and consistent application of appropriate means to achieve a fixed purpose. This purpose itself does not come into question with rational action, in other words, it is unproblematic to it. Someone can act rationally without having any judgement of his own as to whether the purpose he himself serves is a good or a reprehensible one. Rationality is the mode of operation in our 'worlds of work,' the institutions. We also speak in this way, for example, when explaining the rationality of financial borrowing or the rationality of a business model.

Reason, however, is something more than rationality. We are reasonable when we place the purposes presented to us in their wider context and ask whether these are legitimate, whether they are the *right* purposes. Reasonable thinking answers the question of what is *really and not only apparently* of value to us as human beings, and what is therefore worth fighting for. The value concepts that we entertain consciously or unconsciously are the yardstick we apply in the process of criticism (i.e., of conscious differentiation) to the suggested purposes that our society presents to us.

We say, for example, that someone who strictly works through the necessary preliminaries of his next job promotion is behaving rationally. On the other hand, we call someone reasonable who discusses the alternatives of promotion or parental leave with his family and who weighs such factors as family time, childrearing, income, the preferences of family members, etc. when making his decision.

In this sense, Ernst Cassirer calls "reason" a "concept not of a being but of a doing": "Its most important function is its power to bind and to release." (The formulation of "binding and releasing" is not accidental; Cassirer chooses it because it precisely echoes the Catholic doctrine according to which only an ordained priest of the Catholic Church has this power in this earthly domain.) Bonding and dissolving, Cassirer continues, is accomplished by reason in a twofold movement. In the first step, reason *dissolves* the given, be it, for example, a tradition, convention or supposedly divine revelation, into its components. Today we would call this process analysis.

In Cassirer's view, the decisive function of reason lies in the second step. For it is here that the elements we have encountered in our analysis are newly combined and possibly abridged or expanded, *according to new rules*, following a design of our own making and intention. After the disassembly, the analysis, follows the new composition, the synthesis. This ordering principle of our own invention, according to which we review, structure, reject or accept the results of our analysis, thus appropriating them for our intellect – this ordering principle I view as an expression of our self. Nothing characterizes a person as clearly as his thoughts (and also, possibly, their absence). Reasonable thinking brings our values to bear. It establishes our presence in the world as moral persons, i.e., as potential creators of a better reality.

The self of man is *the reason of his life*; not in the *causal* sense in which a passing car is the reason for my distraction, but in the sense that our self is the *rationale*, the 'Whence and Whereto' of our life. The sin against reason therefore lies in the neglect of the self in favor of the 'worlds of work' in which we must exist. As a moral person, we are never completely absorbed in any one of the many 'worlds of work' in which we may find ourselves, whether it be in pursuing our education, serving in the military, working in gainful employment, or whatever other context we may enter: We can evaluate the goals we are pursuing and, where necessary, reject them, because we know how to ask for what is *actually* good and how to hold the purposes we are being guided by up to this standard. In this sense, we are *in* but always also beyond our work environments - if and when we choose to exercise our mind about them, we are intellectually and spiritually superior to them.

Living in reality

The exercise of reason is philosophy - it is the authentic, characteristic activity of moral persons who form and shape themselves over time. As far as we reflect and act reasonably, we exercise our reservation to the thinking and doing in the world, which we have described in the second chapter as the core of morality. In the exercise of reason, a moral person of integrity keeps his own future and the future of society *open*. Thanks to our reasoning capacity, things can be different from what they are because we are consciously in touch with what is real.

Reality is what all parts bring forth through their mutual relations - what arises *on the whole* from what is pursued individually. Therefore, different people know reality to varying degrees, while no one knows it completely. But it is open to exploration. Sophistication is therefore not a question of literacy or intelligence. It is measured by a person's determination to see things *in their context* and to view reality *as a whole*; the measure of intellectual limitation is the unwillingness to do so. Our struggle against the thoroughgoing structuring of our existence by the 'world of work' is, in this sense, our struggle not to be idiots. (The absence of such a struggle proves that someone is an idiot.)

Understanding reality requires a web of considerations that support and enrich each other. This fabric should not be static, but must constantly absorb new experience and generate new questions in order to remain alive. We understand ourselves amidst our life's process by retelling our story and further developing it through new insights and new experiences. In this process, we also make value judgments about what is really worthy of our best efforts; this is how we give our life its direction. In the same way, only collectively, free societies, like most Western European democracies, determine their identity through their political process; and by thwarting precisely this process in various ways, corrupt oligarchies like Russia, China, Brazil and the United States of America ensure the rule of their upper classes.

A friend once explained to me that it is the purpose of a corporation to do things better - that is, to carry out a known process or model evermore efficiently. This is how money is made with the current business model. In life, on the other hand, it's all about 'doing better things' - deciding what would be even better, and pursuing it. He is right: In order to make the most efficient use of what already exists, it is altogether necessary to completely avoid unpredictable elements such as new experiences or unexpected insights. One has to concentrate wholly on the factors that allow the agreed, established purpose to be achieved. 'You can't manage what you can't measure' is management jargon for this will to simplify and concentrate on predictable variables.

The different rationalities that prevail in our work environments are pragmatic and not realistic; they look toward a certain result, not toward a well-ordered whole. The rationality of a 'world of work,' for example that of the military, is not related to reality. It is *not* about deciding, with a view to the social whole, whether the purposes of the military, war preparations and, if ordered, war, should be pursued at all, and if so, to what extent and with what priority. No institution is concerned with reasonable reflection.

On the contrary, the pragmatic rationality of an institution is about making the specific aim of the institution the sole measure of what is undertaken. Every institution, once established, unfolds this dynamic in its social environment. This is why Dwight D. Eisenhower, in his farewell address as U.S. president, warned that the 'military-industrial complex' built up for the Cold War threatened to gain an illegitimate, dominant influence upon American politics. Former US President Eisenhower was aware of the tendency of purpose-oriented institutions to shield their respective goals from relativizing and complicating considerations in order to secure their existence and maximize their influence. The pragmatic rationality of each institution is about simple, schematically defined patterns of thought and behavior. Pragmatism is the intention to disregard reality and reason in order to achieve what is desired.

Reason, on the other hand, has in mind the whole, the *properly ordered* whole: has in mind for ourselves a fruitful life, for our society justice, and for the planet peace and ecological balance. Rationality only seeks the given purpose, if necessary, at the expense of other purposes and in open competition with them. The self, society and planet earth, in other words, *reality*, is the object of reason; function and institution, in other words, the 'worlds of work,' are the object of rationality. Our concern for ourselves, for our society and for our planet is our concern for what is real - for what actually determines our own destiny and that of our community. We are in the world, we are realists, we are alive, only insofar as we care for what is real.

Our concern for our function and for the institution in which we operate is not related to reality, but to a partial world. We are pragmatists and not realists, as far as we concern ourselves with it. It follows that, as functionaries of institutions, we together create the reality that is our industrialized world, and that, at the same time, we make it for one another a dark, if not completely unrecognizable thing. A determined undertaking of enlightenment about ourselves and the ruling forces of our present is necessary to lift this veil. The necessary learning and reflection must be wrested from the strict schedule of our everyday life. Incidentally, the vast majority of people finds itself subject to a strong incentive *not* to do this work - because people are not paid for intellectuality, but for 'just doing it.'

Our current life practice, fixed on reputation and status, with its guiding principles and typical conformism, creates an atmosphere in which our reflectiveness and, with it, our morality are hardly activated and seldom challenged. Our actions as functionaries of industrial society generate evil effects and at the same time hide these effects from us; the 'worlds of work' that we inhabit individually conceal our common reality. The order of prestige and its coalition with the new churches, our purpose-bound institutions, led us into a state of moral poverty. It is easy for us to function for others, and difficult for us to live for ourselves.

7 Professionalism and the management of 'human capital'

Integration into the world of work offers relief from our insecurity and general spiritual homelessness. Rational work and an associated cult of professionalism and success are offered to us as an ordering principle for our whole life - as redemption in success. This offer seems realistic and plausible owing to the usual disorientation experienced by a person who has learned to function in the order of prestige.

In the deepest depths of our being, we have been accustomed to considering the presumed expectations of others, with anxious attention, and we constantly unsettle ourselves with this. Just as a bat steers this way and that according to the signals it receives from its sonar, we avoid collisions and chaos as best we can by means of a long-practiced social discipline. Those who have become nimble and adept in this practice may draw their small triumphs of everyday life from this proficiency; but this does not mean that they have overcome their disorientation. It only means that they practice their conformism with a smile and occasionally give themselves a pat on the back.

Most people find a sense of security and reassurance in the reliable, largely calculable expectations placed upon us by those institutions that need us as their pragmatic functionaries. But reality remains hidden from us in our role as functionaries, i.e., from the inner perspective of every 'world of work.'. The peculiar social and psychological rearing of its members creates a mentality that renders industrial society incapable of adequate self-perception. Individual students of the order of status and prestige are distracted from working on themselves in the light of experience, i.e., from life itself; the institutional form of industrial society adds another dimension of dissociation from reality.

This is the present, our social playground and minefield. In its coordinate system we have to find our path in life, *which must not simply be a career in our 'worlds of work.'* That is easy to say and must seem presumptuous at this point: Who am I to say, and how do I know what is and what is not sufficient to give our lives purpose and meaning? By what yardstick do I measure this, and why should one accept my standards? After the diagnosis of the present, we will proceed in this section to take two further intellectual steps that taken together better enable us to answer the question "What now?" in the final chapter.

The first step is to shed light on the difficult relationship between professionalism and leadership in our work environments. Choosing this focus has a certain philosophical advantage: professionalism is expected *of all of us* as the operational discipline of our institution. And *all of us* are subjected to others' leadership, or are ourselves exercising leadership over others. At all levels *below* the head of an authority or company, a leader is both subject *and* object of leadership activity; one 'is a boss *and* has a boss.' Accordingly, if we focus on professionalism and leadership, we can talk in reference to *all of us* and also about the logic and atmosphere in which we actually spend long periods of our daily lives together. And talking about *all of us* (with due caution) is the claim and the task of a philosophy that wants to be helpful for life.

In addition, modern institutions are also subject to a specific dilemma, the influence of which makes the conceptual pairing of professionalism and leadership even more relevant to this philosophy. For institutions need professionalism *and* leadership, and the one force, by its very nature, counteracts the other. Institutions need stable, regular operations and a clear discipline based on the division of labor to manage their day-to-day business. There must therefore be an element of practically blind obedience, in normal operations, so that what is required does not have to be renegotiated every day. This discipline of daily business, of steady-state operations, is called "professionalism."

It is preached, taught and practiced in our administrations and companies as a quasi-morality because it guarantees the functioning of the system. And the fruits of this system are indispensable and desirable in many respects. But in much the same way, our institutions need qualified leadership that is capable of recurringly breaking down the system of obedience that professionalism represents, and adapting it to new circumstances. An institution must be able to disrupt and reform itself in order to survive the constant changes in its environment. We will critically analyze professionalism and leadership, but this does not call into question their necessity. Crucial to the train of thought in this book is that the interaction of these two factors creates an everyday experience of inhibited and distorted humanity.

And it is, to be sure, this characteristic everyday experience in our 'worlds of work' that leads in the end to the second main point of the reflection in this chapter. For this experience generates a tremendous demand for the complete scrapping of independent reflection. From this arises an equally formidable, pressing demand for a theory of exoneration that seems to justify our moral self-abandonment: industrial society, especially its 'officers' of all ranks, needs an intellectual alibi for its complete and immensely impactful indifference in an obviously unjust world. Only the pseudo-philosophy of moral relativism has such an alibi to offer. This is why a majority of us has adopted it wholeheartedly, often with an intellectual sigh of relief.

Professionalism as liberating obedience

It is always to be understood as praise when someone is attested professionalism in the working world. It is the learned ability to fully engage in a trade, in a function, and to disregard other impulses and considerations at work, - at least in terms of the idea and the tendency of behavior –, however important those impulses are to the person in other respects. The professional treats himself and others as 'human capital,' as a factor in the process of production. This must always remain an uncomfortable, precarious undertaking, no matter how much one is trained in it.

For I myself and the people I deal with actually *always* remain full moral persons with their own dignity; they are not 'human capital.' Through a deliberate and programmatic reversal of the facts, industrial society treats us as something we are not. Professionalism therefore produces distorted humanity - an inhibited form of interpersonal interaction reduced to rigid patterns. One characteristic of this peculiar way of dealing with people is its aspect of *thoughtlessness-by-design*.

This may sound like an extravagant contrivance, but *planned thoughtlessness* is actually demonstrated in our industrial everyday lives over and over again. For example, it comes to light in the fact that professional observers expect other professionals to deliver the operational work required of them with an unwavering constancy, unencumbered by questions or concerns. (In the sense that no questions are actually asked and something specific is simply carried out - *not* in the sense that professionals of all occupations *have* no questions.) Let us look at when and how a perceived *lack of* professionalism is criticized, in order to see this move more clearly. It always happens in the aftermath of an observed behavior, and then mostly in the tone of a final verdict: "That was totally unprofessional!" One assumes among professionals that the other should have known better in advance of the situation under consideration, and should have either prevented it or defused it easily.

There is nothing to ask, and the gesture of criticism is, accordingly, that the delinquent is 'surprising' his co-workers with his ignorance of an obvious requirement. As an everyday business move, this gesture is not implausible: After all, regulations, administrative procedures, work protocols, and job descriptions, as well as compliance guidelines and institutional values exist, *by definition*, to relieve our everyday activities of uncertainties and of the need for case-by-case interpretation. Hence, following the logic and self-image of the system, in any case, one *can* actually 'wonder' why anyone at all would *not* act according to instructions, and thus 'professionally.' This is, then, the opportune diplomatic form of complaint about it.

However, it is *not* established practice in everyday business to examine oneself and others to see what considerations might have overridden the usual operational reasons this time. After all, this possibility of being convinced by *better reasons is* not something one would expect in daily operations. This makes the authoritarian structure of the situation apparent: To behave professionally means to calculate in operational, and exclusively operational terms, to weigh one's steps, and, finally, to take them toward the sole end, namely, the efficient and effective execution of established practices for accepted ends. We are then rational, i.e., devoted to the purpose of the business, and not reasonable. The reasonable question as to what it is that we have the best reasons to do and therefore *should* do, does not appear on the agenda in professional business.

There, based on the professional business agenda, something is decided and done with respect to the purpose of the institution, as communicated to us by our superiors. We do not ask what reasons there are in favor and against this purpose of the company, or how, in this or that situation, other considerations may justly supersede it. When in doubt, we act unreasonably with rational intent, even though we are beings endowed with reason. In this sense, professionalism is the opposite of humanity, it is the acquired '*industriality,*' or the studied *self-mechanization* of man; in yet other words, professionalism is the craft of the functionary, the opposite of the craft of life. In this sense, Hannah Arendt remarked in a conversation held in 1964 with Joachim Fest that "the real perversion of action [...] is functioning."

For reflective people, professionalism raises a suspicion of falsehood and human inadequacy. People who are professionally cooperating and also leading other people, create for one other in a steady, uninterrupted flow this moral inconvenience of our institutions. In the performing arts, this perception of an unnatural one-sidedness in our work environment is reflected in parodies, satires and especially in a certain genre of films in which individuals, contrary to the logic of their role in the operation, put aside the forms and procedures to simply provide help from person to person – or, alas, run amok. These exceptions confirm the rule of unquestioned conformism, and they reveal the longing that these exceptions may yet become the rule. A system characterizes itself by the fantasies of escape and overcoming that it gives rise to.

But what, then, in view of this section's title, does professionalism have to do with 'liberation'? In what sense can the obedience of professional work be understood as 'liberating'? Behind the cult of quasi-moral 'professionalism,' there is a consequent, unsentimental understanding of the requirements of industrial operations - but also an equally clear concept of the needs of the working individual. Thinking this through also brings out the freedom-serving, humane aspect of professionalism.

Without a fundamental narrowing of perspective and disciplining of our sensibilities, industrial society cannot endure. Professionalism is a *systemic requirement of* this society - but not only to secure the large, interdependent complex of industrial business. For in the details of operation, *every* function that industrial society presents us with is in principle equally unrelated to the future prospects of *each* individual who may be carrying it out. Therefore, there are (except in the case of a few particularly inspired people) no compelling reasons to choose a particular function. Realistically, one should not assume a deeply felt vocation or a content-related fascination of the individual with regard to the purpose and operational details of a particular institution.

Therefore, from a social point of view, every possible function *must* be made available to everyone: Otherwise it would be impossible to attain to a sufficient number of functionaries for the various institutions. However, it is just as important to take the individual into account. Without 'functional flexibility' and a principle of permeability in the professional order, employees who are not especially inspired by a deep interest in the subject matter of their job would have a hard time making a living. Industrial society as a system has an existential need for this general interchangeability of functionaries, as does modern man as its inhabitant. Our professionalism guarantees this interchangeability and also, by the same token, a certain degree of individual freedom amidst the struggle for a livelihood.

Industrial society requires professionalism for its own survival, and it offers us a livelihood in return. It is therefore absolutely necessary that professionalism be considered a virtue and be propagated as such. However, it is the exact opposite of a virtue. For a virtue is the path to an important good of life, taught over many generations through experience and observation. Therefore, whoever has a virtue has at least *once* thought for himself - when he decided that a certain attitude and practice is worth learning and cultivating in order to attain a certain good in life.

By contrast, professionalism is purposeful, consciously ordered thoughtlessness. It does not require thought but only obedience to instructions, and accordingly it does not produce virtues but only habits. What some people may erroneously consider to be the 'virtue' of professionalism, is in reality, from a moral point of view, merely the observance of a rule of prudence: "Professionalize yourself at least in *some* discipline, otherwise things can easily get dicey for you economically!"

For reliably acting strictly within the bounds of institutional rationality – i.e., for unreasonable behavior -, the industrial system repays us by guaranteeing our substitutability. A functionary of one institution can tomorrow be the functionary of another. In the same way, one can take on other tasks within an institution (and certainly outside the framework of one's previous knowledge, as well). A top manager once told me with a hearty laugh that he was now a marketing manager, without ever having represented a product, and that he would soon be taking over an IT department.

In such an environment, the individual has every reason to strive to be – in Kant's oddly entertaining expression - "fit for every saddle," to be able to learn every role, to remain permanently elastic and yielding ('flexible'), to practice "life-long learning," as our politicians like to say. The system, on the other hand, must strive to maintain the actual substitutability of all by all in order to survive.

The ideal of economic equality of opportunity cannot only be justified on humanistic grounds; it is an ideal that maintains the architecture and the balance of power within the industrial system. The political struggle for opportunities to participate, the anti-discrimination laws and company programs to address discrimination against this or that group, the complication of language through gender-neutral expressions, and the complication of everyday life through 'neutralistic' dress codes - all this serves the system *and* its members at the same time. The progressive differentiation regarding the protection of minorities, with its cautious modes of speech and behavior, is at once both social discipline *and* individual liberation.

As an important consequence, the political discussion is distracted from considering of general problems such as economic inequality, which could be unpleasant for the winners of the current industrial system to discuss in depth. Meanwhile, politicians and activists who struggle for "gender-neutral" toilet facilities and want to make grammar "non-discriminatory" do not get in the way of the economic rulers of industrial society with an unwelcome articulation of demands for a more equitable participation of everyone in the prosperity generated by everyone.

"The dominant idea is one in which social justice is essentially synonymous with non-discrimination" (Walter Benn Michaels). The fact that several million people in Germany and proportionately even more people in the United States can no longer live adequately on the income provided by a full-time job hardly seems to be recognizable as a problem of justice, from this point of view. Obscenely unequal distribution of wealth, which undermines democratic equality, is not objected to if it is not due to discrimination against some specific group.

It is undisputed, however, that this mindset regarding our manners and ways of speaking, call it 'strained political sterility' (rather than 'political correctness'), improves the individual's chances to secure his material livelihood even if no particular interests or passions animate his professional activity. Systematic discrimination on the basis of my membership in certain population groups is becoming less likely, and that is significant and morally important: for everyone must 'earn his living.' The right not to be discriminated against is also the individual's right to at least *some kind of* professionalism. One must be able to become in some way a resource of the system in order to survive.

It appears perfectly consistent with this analysis that employees of institutions are seen and treated as human capital ('human resources') of their company, i.e., as functionaries and not simply as people. However, this approach marks a clear, fundamental injustice of the industrial system. The ideological degradation of human beings to a means of production is against the law in Germany, because it obviously contradicts the foundational principle of the German constitution that "human dignity is inviolable." Wanting to use a human being as a company 'resource' is in all seriousness just as impermissible as using him as a 'human shield' in war.

Nevertheless, the brutal expression 'human resource' is fully accepted in the personnel departments of our companies and administrations. I am not aware of any constitutional complaints against such use of the term; the consensus (or thoughtlessness) seems solid. But let's think this through: what could a 'human resource' possibly be? People use resources, that is, means, for the ends that they have devised for themselves. How could humans themselves serve as a 'resource'? Well, human bodies could be used as a resource.

Unfortunately, this is no absurd or ridiculous proposition. Human beings have been traded as objects in the context of slavery. In the early phase of industrialization, in Europe in particular, workers were literally physically consumed, and this is still happening to differing degrees in the so-called 'low-income countries.' Soap has been made from human bones, human heads have been shrunk into trophies and human hair has been used as a resource. And frequently, human bodies are still used in war, as a resource of imperial politics, just like any other material.

Let us assume for our purposes, however, that we do not mean the term 'human resources' in that sense. If, however, it is not to be our bodies that serve as 'human resources,' then this expression must refer to that which resides in the human body. It has to do with the abilities and skills of people who are to be brought into the operational process of production in some way. This is what "human resource" (HR) departments and managers make their business. They don't want to cut people to pieces and then process their body parts, they want to use the skills and abilities of employees in a targeted way for the purpose of the production of goods and services. (On a psychological level, however, this may be seen as analogous to the fragmentation and processing of the body, depending on the management system applied in the process.)

This economy of skills and abilities also includes the planned promotion and development of skills and abilities among those who appear capable of improving. Psychology and group dynamics play a role in this, as do organizational and planning issues. From the point of view of industrial society, human beings are therefore regarded as an operating resource to be managed and controlled: That is the meaning of 'human resource management,' the activation and purposeful direction of human abilities and skills.

Leadership is the art of change

Managing employees is therefore a complex business that not just anyone is capable of executing; leadership is not just any job. In addition to blind obedience (i.e., professionalism), it is one of two functions without which an institution cannot survive. Why this is so becomes clear by way of a small detour via Charles Darwin. Darwin developed his theory of evolution with view to the individual organism: New species emerge because sometimes individual organisms exhibit small variations from their parent generation. Because of their small peculiarities, these creatures sometimes have a slightly higher probability to reproduce than the 'normal' members of their generation. This is because the environment is always changing, creating new needs for adaptation by the species living in it.

These new environmental requirements are now opportunities for "deviators" to assert themselves. If the temperature in a habitat drops, those animals that happen to be born with a slightly thicker coat of fur than their conspecifics have slightly better chances of survival. They are slightly more likely to have offspring than their generation-mates without untypically thick fur. Thus, this small deviation continues into the next generation and may over many generations become a characteristic of a new species. The process of nature is not the repetition of the same, but the emergence of the new. It is only the slowness of this constant revolution of all things combined with the brevity of our life span that disguises this to us.

Institutions, like companies and administrations, are not living beings, but nevertheless there is a clear parallel. The survival of an institution depends on its ability to respond to change in its environment; its survival is a matter of its making appropriate adjustments in its way of working that take account of these environmental changes. For example, a company that stays with index cards and paper documents instead of digitizing its records and making them flexible to processing builds up a dangerous cost disadvantage in relation to its competitors. Its customers will not compensate for this backwardness in the long run by paying comparatively higher prices.

A society that does not take action against environmental degradation such as increasing insect mortality or microplastics will suffer consequential damage that can be irreparable and disastrous for its own survival. Leadership is the work of bringing about changes that are recognized as necessary. It is therefore instructive to think of leadership as essentially a kind of crisis activity. The crisis in question always consists in the fact that an established way of working and its established procedures no longer does justice to changed environmental conditions.

It is not necessary for a mistake to have been made, for such a need for change to arise. Much to the contrary, it is usually the case that many people have simply 'done everything right' for a long time, in the sense of their established professionalism, overlooking a need for change. Anyone doing his work according to a given pattern or process *must* ultimately always look at the tasks he faces as if they fit into his pattern or process. After all, this is usually the case. Those who have learned to swing a hammer will see nails everywhere and will not of their own accord pull out a screwdriver. If they did, that would be punished as 'unprofessional.' After all, there were reasons for giving them a hammer and nails; it seemed expedient.

The manager who has identified a need for change, i.e., a crisis of current professionalism, must initiate and organize the response to it. After all, professionals do not initiate change, they always carry on as usual. What is needed is a crisis of change in which one professionalism is transformed into another, modified one. Leadership has its daily business, its very own professionalism. Leading means professionally breaking through established professionalism and reorganizing it.

The functionaries undergo realignment, they learn a new way of working so that the operation becomes better suited to the conditions defined for it by a changing outside world. He who is in a leadership role is of necessity also a functionary, but a special one: the functionary whose function is the (re)orientation of functionaries. Our leader is thus appointed to reform our work environment. He has the task of influencing us thoroughly in this process of adaptation.

Who can lead?

But who leads? It is not enough to answer: "The boss, of course." For the formal role that a person holds in an organization does not allow for any conclusion to be drawn as to whether he is leading. Whoever wants to lead, must either have enough depth and originality of self to relate to other people and understand them. Or he must at least be able to fake this until he is promoted to a leadership role. Young people in high positions usually belong to this latter category of dazzlers, because depth and originality of the self develop over time, with the intelligent and humble processing of manifold experiences. These qualities of the self do not emerge over the course of studying business administration and, e.g., the compulsory subject "Strategic Management", and emerge only to a modest degree in the marathon of internship and volunteering that is run by ambitious CV-optimizers.

Where they are selected (and not simply pushed forward on the basis of irrelevant considerations, such as acquaintance, networking, gender or attractiveness), leaders are recruited on the basis of their apparent ability to maintain pleasant human relations with employees and their co-leaders. From the middle management level in an institution upwards, the mission is simply to build trust in every horizontal and vertical direction. This is consistent because the normal case is mistrust that competition for scarce goods (such as leadership positions) necessarily generates. Trustful cooperation is indeed the most effective way to be able to use others whenever necessary in the interest of the operation and to align their actions and thoughts.

Management is the goal-oriented administration of a structure made up of employees and their clearly regulated work processes; leadership, in turn, is the *alignment of* people which the leader has to master. (This distinction is not mine, but appears in various forms in the leadership literature of many authors). The manager directs, the leader aligns; one stabilizes patterns, the other breaks them. Having managers at the top in crisis situations is a life-threatening danger for every company, every administration, every country. Managers need leadership, they usually do not exercise it. For they represent the status quo, the established professionalism.

Aligning employees and an entire organization with its subdivisions to a new purpose is almost an alchemy. Leaders have to be pensive to be up to this task; it can be said without mystical pathos that in the person of the leader, the system thinks about itself: To exert influence, the leader *must* generally want to know how the system works and how it influences his colleagues. Without this insight, a leader cannot navigate, and fails in the craft of leading even before he can begin to exercise it.

For every crisis of change apparently has clearly 'factual' aspects on the one hand and just as clearly 'human' aspects on the other. In truth, these cannot be clearly separated from one another. They form a disorderly, incalculable whole, which can only be partially cleared up in any one individual case through intensive involvement in the surrounding circumstances and human emotions of the concrete situation. This or that new technology, for example, has to be introduced for compelling objective reasons; some established ways of working are thus to be abolished or replaced by new processes. In human terms, this means stress, which in clinical terms is nothing other than the physical and psychological reaction to change.

Frightened, insecure people are now discussing the allegedly "purely factual questions" of, say, a particular change in technology. And this emotional fact alone transforms these technological questions into problems of psychology and even group dynamics. And these are often very unpleasant to deal with - such that weak leaders do not like to face and help shape them, but prefer instead to allow these to take a chaotic course, all the while paying careful attention not to be stuck with direct responsibility for the attendant results. A high proportion of all processes of change, perhaps 70%, regularly fail precisely because of this.

For this reason, strategically reflecting on all interested parties, consciously taking risks, and no less consciously accepting frictions and conflicts play the decisive role in the implementation of change. Without a willingness to accept these conditions, leadership cannot be exercised. Intellectually, one must wish to know how specific colleagues who are important for change in question can be influenced. And interpersonally, one must be able to actually find that out.

In a superficial, misleading interpretation of this predicament, it is really about putting oneself in other people's shoes to then be able to better *manipulate* them. It is, however, a matter of understanding in each case what is rational from their point of view, and, where possible, of showing that the reasonableness of one's own project takes these established purposes into consideration and does not deliberately harm them. Sociability, compassion, understanding of social dynamics and an honest interest in others suddenly become indispensable *as tools of leadership*. If you are met in this way with a friendly manner by your manager, this is not, as you should know, *only* because of your own kindness and likability.

The whole person, the whole personality of the leader is challenged in instigating and working through crises of change. It is a business that, if it is really *conducted* and not only conveniently *feigned*, is unlikely to bring its protagonists general popularity. Intellectual acuity, diligence and assertiveness - qualities that are often and rightly associated with leadership - only lead to career progress up to a certain point.

Great leaders can be recognized by the serenity and strength of personality by which they allow the full meaning and utility of the contributions of others to unfold. But this is not the usual case: The higher up in an organization the people having to decide on the next promotion of others are situated, the more status anxiety they often feel themselves. And the more difficult they find it, for example, to give the groundbreaking ideas of others the space they deserve, without imagining themselves 'humiliated' or their own position threatened.

The secret of those most successful in hierarchical advancement is, accordingly, that they usually do not lead at all. They do *not* decisively implement changes that have been recognized as necessary. Instead, they make themselves popular with those currently in power and cultivate their network. The really effective leaders are busy challenging the establishment, not joining it.

This is why ineffective leaders often end up in top positions; particularly those who cause little offense because they question little and who thus hardly trigger the release of stress hormones in others because they produce little change. Fast careers (except for strokes of luck) are often explained by leadership failure, or by the cynical simulation of decisive action while painful decisions in detail are carefully avoided.

Moral pitfalls of change

Actually implementing change means getting into a kind of moral twilight that most leaders would not enter if they could only avoid it. A leader must have the intellectual capacity for all kinds of differentiated, well-calibrated moves in social space. In a professionalized world, a strategist - i.e., a person who thinks reasonably and not just rationally, and is therefore well-suited to lead - can only be someone who recognizes the mentally and emotionally restrictive influence of professionalism on himself and others, and who is capable of adjusting his behavior accordingly.

The strategist must avoid contracting the occupational disease of professionalism. Capable leaders are aware of the blinders that professionalism puts on others and potentially on themselves. They must find a language that acknowledges this limited perspective without confirming it. Only on this basis can functionaries be given a new orientation, an 'updated' version of their professionalism that makes it functional under changed circumstances.

In the crisis situation of change, the simple, 'undosed' truth is therefore usually not a practicable option; a calculating handling of information and opinions cannot be avoided. (I write here quite consciously "of information and opinions" - *not* "of facts." Whoever lies has ruined his credibility as soon as the facts come to light. Honesty is not only morally required to safeguard people's integrity as well as one's own. It is also the only promising policy of change, in the long run.)

The basic situation of exercising leadership is always delicate right from the start: If, as a leader, I say that the current professionalism of the institution is no longer in tune with the outside environment – then, following the logic of the system, I am simply demonstrating my lack of professionalism. Because, as we will be informed, "The sales organization was set up with a strong sales force in regions X and Y because the success of product development in recent years made it necessary to build up this capacity"; "The centralization of application processing in a single 'service center' follows the industry trend"; "We finally had to follow the US trend towards *Business Design Innovation Excellence Reengineering*, and so we set up a streamlined department for this purpose," etc. This reaction is understandable. After all, recent experience points to the correctness, indeed, the necessity of exactly the form of professionalism that is currently practiced: "We are doing things this way, and we are still here, so it must be right!"

However, while we are contentedly sitting at our desk or in our armchair, the world we are used to may very well already have disappeared. The strategist must recognize that this insight is naturally frightening to employees, and he must take this emotional fact seriously. More than 500 years ago, Niccolò Machiavelli – frequently and quite unfairly cast as a cold theorist of sheer power play - noted why even employees who are among the winners *of change* are not very reliable allies *in change*: "Those who introduce new laws make enemies of all those who were comfortable with the previous ones, and only very lukewarm friends with those who stand to benefit from the new laws." For the winners of the new order have not yet experienced it, it remains for the time being only a weak promise with little motivational effect.

If a leader wants to establish new behaviors in the face of this completely human fear of change and the persistence of professional habit, he must 'diplomatize' the process. Plans and events must be interpreted for the parties involved, in such a way that they are not cheated, but can still hear the right thing at the right time and therefore go along with it.

An original, insightful image that Thomas S. Kuhn uses in his book on the Copernican Revolution illustrates the nature of a leadership task. According to Kuhn's metaphor, people must be guided *through a curve* to move from the Aristotelian idea that the earth stands still, with the sun circling around it, to Copernicus' reverse view: If you stand on the road and look towards the bend, the road just seems to end with that bend. But if one looks at the situation from the apex of the curve, one can look back in the one direction to his old view of the fixed earth, and also appreciate its justification. But from the vertex, one can also see the part of the road that follows after the bend and leads into the heliocentric world view.

According to this allegory, it is important for the leader of a change process to bring new aspects into the discussion and make new arrangements in comprehensible steps; this is how the inclination of the straight road into curve begins. Something new becomes plausible step by step, without a shout of "Revolution!" in the sense of: "Your road ends here!" At the appropriate time, the determination of which depends solely on the judgement of the leader, a 'transformation story' can then be told: "We come from *this* view and practice. It had good reasons in its favor, and has helped us achieve a lot. We are now following a different approach for the reasons we worked through together, and are going in a different direction."

This message can be sent and understood at the vertex of the change curve, given that the impulses for change have previously been dosed and timed intelligently. Kuhn's image teaches that any existing professionalism, the blind obedience of an institutional crew, can only be reoriented step by step. The leader of a change process cannot always explain and discuss the intended transformation in full detail *as a change process*. Then he would overwhelm the employees and undermine his rapport with them; not because they could not follow *intellectually*, but because *as people* with a natural aversion to uncertainty, they would then be *practically* unable to follow.

In addition to these psychological factors, the forces acting in the established structure would also lead to the immediate blocking of the change effort. This is the case because established professionalism is always right *by definition*, and its representatives hold decisive power in the current structure. A leader must therefore act pragmatically according to the guiding principles of his program for change and win over others to join him in doing the same. The path to change does *not* lead via an intellectual conviction shared by everyone about the correctness of certain views, but via the actions of some, which create a growing dynamic until - to speak with Kuhn - the apex of the curve has been reached together.

Once this point has been reached through skillful guidance, the architects of change suddenly start to *benefit* from the strictly rational focus placed by our institutions on limited purposes. It is then quite sufficient to demonstrate that the positive business results are a consequence of the new approach, in order to move beyond scandal - "He's questioning our professionalism! – to a state in which everyone is certain to have already known for a long time that the new direction was the only viable option all along.

Nevertheless, the craft of leadership remains delicate even in this phase. The path to an *accepted* change leads through concrete, verifiable improvements, and on that path, one is bound to step on many toes - of those who had power in the status quo but who did not themselves achieve this success. For they may not have recognized the opportunity or the need for change. Or they may have recognized it but did not dare to take the risk of driving change for fear of failing and suffering consequences for their career.

It is therefore important for managers to expect to encounter cowardice and stupidity within their environment. This does not mean that our cooperation partners in institutions *are* cowardly and stupid; it only means that a leader who acts in such a way that cowardly and stupid people will resist out of fear, significantly reduces his chances of success. You do not have to be misanthropic, but what is said and done must, if possible, leave the weakest link in the desired chain of effects unbothered until, so to speak, the dispute has been resolved *without a dispute.* Here we have a taste of the moral twilight of the work of change that we mentioned before.

In a significant transformative process, the mosaic pieces of concrete improvements result in a completely different way of working with new demands placed upon the employees, perhaps even in a completely different organization. However, with skillful leadership, this is not discussed in a grand manner or in academic breadth: It becomes clear to a few intellectuals here and there as they reflect on the scene, and still later, in retrospect, to a few more sensible people.

Most stakeholders, however, are simply guided around Kuhn's curve through the stepwise administration of reasonable, though sometimes unwelcome demands.. They glide over into a new professionalism - a professionalism that they never quite saw coming and which they can accept precisely because they were not asked to judge its shape and form too soon. They were simply, and quite literally, introduced to it, led into it.

The permanent moral crisis of leadership

Owing to the difficulties and pitfalls of their work for their own emotional life and moral integrity, leaders in our institutions enjoy limited privileges - especially the privilege of being taken into consideration as full personalities. Those who for operational profits are not simply to *have* their humanity, but also to *employ it* in a calculated manner, even in the finer ramifications of human relations, must also be perceived and promoted by the institution in the entirety of their person. In order to make a human being as *manager* into a resource for an institution, his personality *must* be taken seriously; otherwise, it will never be possible to put it fully into service.

This circumstance makes it possible for people of a more pensive character to find for themselves a niche in industrial operations. One can rightly imagine that one's own progress as a leader involves a progressive development of one's own personality, that is, provided that one wants to see an ever greater versatility of behaviors, an ever more virtuous ability to adapt from situation to situation, and an increasingly supple exercise of power, as a growing degree of maturity. In any case, one receives the opportunity to become more experienced and knowledgeable in all aspects of dealing with people, and also to experience with them many beautiful and ugly things.

Superiors, for example, often receive training based on systems theory for conceiving of the employee as a system of motivations; he has to be docked onto for being put in a "performance mood." The most efficient way to do this is to actively 'manage' the interpersonal and nervous damages of a professionalized work environment. For example, one acts in a compensatory, palliative, almost overly appreciative manner, one clings to a kind of schoolyard cheerfulness in groups, before getting down to business, in order to then be able to assert oneself there.

The leader's professionalism consists in making and keeping the 'human capital,' the functionaries, productive, by means of the well-calculated *use* of humaneness, authenticity, attention, encouragement, praise and 'constructive' rebuke, overstatement, temporary concealment, moderation or exaggeration. Anyone who has ever seen a manager begin his presentation with a personal anecdote and opening arm movements(*by no means* closing) knows what I am talking about.

Leadership is always and exclusively about influencing other people in a well-thought-out way. In order to be effective, the supervisor must be able to play the claviature of interpersonal situations competently. He must be able to build trust with many different people in many different situations and ensure their constructive cooperation. At any given time, it is only a small step from legitimate influence to downright deceitful manipulation.

The boundary is always fluid in the practice of leadership, for example, when one asks: Who needs to hear what message in which key, so that under the conditions of his particular perspective and interests he is able to get with the program? What information needs to be communicated, to be touched upon, or to be left out temporarily or completely? Which depth of conversation, at which moment, in which situation is most expedient?

At what point in a complex process is which step possible with whom, and which step is not yet or no longer possible? What are the dynamics in a room with a group of people with different perspectives on change? By means of what kind of moderation can these dynamics be controlled so that the necessary result can be achieved? How do you deal with obstructionists, refusers and negative comments? Which 'adjutants' do you select for such an event in order to shape the power situation in the group in line with your own intentions? And, last but not least, how as a leader does one remain open to the possibly superior thoughts of others in order to learn from them?

Leadership in institutions is not only about the conscious, situational exercising of influence upon people; it is about influencing their perceptions in a general and methodical manner. While the ambitious employee is busy guessing the conditions for success that his superior defines for him, the superior, for his part, has a lot of work to do in deciding what colleagues of different ranks, respectively, should perceive of him. After all, what they will deem possible and impossible and the degree of cooperation they will show him depend on these perceptions.

All this takes place in a paradoxical situation where employees always know that it is not really about them, but about safeguarding operations under changing circumstances. It is always clear to everyone that under these new circumstances their current job may no longer be needed. That is why the supervisor always knows that his fellow human beings - even if he is completely honest - are always part of a wider, carefully devised game. It is about profit, or, in an administration, about legally compliant operations, and *therefore* it must *also be about* the needs of the employees. Because as 'human capital,' employees are factors of profit like electricity, water, and perhaps bricks and mortar.

Each one is therefore dealt with in the way the supervisor deems necessary to achieve cooperation. The humanity and friendliness that one encounters is never *simply* humanity and friendliness, but must always be seen in the context of its purpose. It never really becomes warm, because everything is just hot air. Whoever wants to praise his superior, says that he is authentic, human, honest, etc. With such assurances, the truth is expressed, only in reverse, as in a shadow cut: the truth that conformism, interpersonal disinterest and an informal approach to the truth are the norm in the world of work. Therefore, any positive deviation from this norm triggers relief and is almost counted as a moral merit.

If possible, one should not work for a superior who lacks awareness of the moral predicament posed by the basic situation in which he has to reflect and act. Unbroken self-confidence in the permanent moral crisis of leadership signals an incomplete perception of one's own situation which may easily become the reason for a lack of compassion.

Remarkably, only a leader who himself cultivates a high degree of sincerity and truthfulness in dealing with himself is able to muster the required, calculating influence. A leader must want to know exactly what the facts of the situation are, what the others are thinking and feeling - and what kind of influence he himself typically exerts on these factors through his personal attributes and habitus.

Broad knowledge of every kind and the highly differentiated self-knowledge that comes with it constitute a leader's capital. Effective leaders have sound judgment based on broad education and consequently a clear awareness of their own impact on others. They are also capable of acknowledging their part in the success or failure of encounters with others, learning from them and, if necessary, making sincere apologies.

All leaders have to work with omission and emphasis, narrowing and and broadening the perspective of their statements as the occasion demands. One could take a strict moralistic stance and call all these operations "lies." But these "lies" told by good leaders are honest in a certain sense: They know themselves and know a lot about their employees, whom they are happy to support and whom they also want to help in a humane way. Still, professionally they can only apply their knowledge to use the employees as a means to the end of the institution. That is professionalism.

There is human directness, authenticity, straightforwardness to be found in many leaders. And precisely the fact that this is the leadership ideal for the most sincere managers makes it clear that the system favors something else. The great lie and perversion that people are treated as resources which they are not and cannot be - this great lie infects the small activities of everyday industrial life; nothing about it should therefore be considered innocent and humanly straightforward.

The lie about the proverbial human 'cog in the wheel' is big enough that, once accepted, it offers room enough for the 'truths' of an entire cast of everyday life. It is this perversion at the bottom of industrial society that makes alternative social models that are more oriented towards participation and community, attractive to humanistically-minded people. An institution in which the dynamics of 'human resource management' would not be able to take hold, would have to be run collectively and as free of hierarchy as possible, i.e., cooperatively.

In order to constantly achieve better-paying positions in the actual institutions of our world of workplaces, the practice (though not necessarily the mentality) of *manipulative relativism* is required: We strive in each moment to be who we think the others need, and we speak a language that ais attuned to this situational diplomacy. "One must have an ulterior motive and, starting from this, one must judge everything, while speaking like the ordinary people" (Blaise Pascal). Every employee is constantly involved in this polite, dosed mutual falsehood.

However, an employee without a leadership role has the privilege of escaping the complete sell-out of his person to the operation with comparative ease. His superior is much more at risk of death by conformism. It suffices for an normal employee, after all, to put on his professionalism like a somewhat stiff suit for a few hours a day. Nobody expects him to engage in the extensive 'relationship management' of a leader, who must, of course, as a functionary, always, throughout the entire human relationship, remain professional. However, employees are expected not to disturb the program by uncoordinated truth telling or with critical questioning.

The Alibi of Relativism

What does it take philosophically, i.e., in reflection, to settle down comfortably in this well-structured, well-regulated falsehood? After all, it is human to entrust one's true feelings and judgments to others who seem to be kindly disposed to me. In working life, however, one constantly follows an agenda of one's own – this is a feature of the system and completely independent of a person's particular character. You influence others according to your own agenda, or you at least keep a productive distance from them. This is not compatible with the development of genuine interpersonal trust.

If we are in our right minds, we will never in the context of industrial operations *fully* trust ourselves or anyone else we encounter there.

Because all interpersonal events in our working environments are morally flimsy. Professionalism is supposed to guarantee that we leave our personal peculiarities unconsidered in our thoughts and actions so that the purpose of the operation does not suffer from our humanity. And everyone knows (if they think about it) that this is an impossibility, a fundamental reversal, i.e., a perversion of human relations under the misleading catchword 'cooperation.'

The theatrical play of our professionalism can therefore only be learned by practicing patterns of interaction - just as one once learned to curtsy at court. Liveliness cannot be removed, it can only be suppressed. The handy checklist for our "application interview" or our "salary negotiation" distracts us from wanting to do things as ourselves - e.g., "bang on the table for once", which is quite logically the main subject of many comedic reappraisals of our world of workplaces.

The aseptic formulas of 'training' and 'mentoring' make it easier for radical functionaries to live with the fact that they have no idiosyncrasies at all. Clever and experienced professionals like to praise each other in the vocabulary of board games: "Well played!" "Good move!" Either way, the theater of professionalism contributes thus to the everyday comfort of industrial existence. And this comfort stabilizes itself, the more people professionalize themselves.

Professionalism is the mildew that grows upon on all pursuits in modern societies. The intentional application of goal-driven rationality *to the highest degree attainable*, means that all of us together are constantly working to trivialize our experiences. In a professionalized world, the momentum and tact, taste and atmosphere of every matter of human interest falls victim to ideological cramps: everyone must be enabled to, in principle, do anything at all, according to objective criteria. Where 'professionalization' has not taken hold, neither operational efficiency nor 'equal opportunities' can be guaranteed. An area that has not been professionalized has not yet been opened up to equal-opportunity economic struggle.

Once settled in the mode of professional humanity, our work routine also provides a stage on which to perform the whole spectrum of human relationship dramas. On the plateau of a gentle mendacity, underscored less by winking than by eye rolls, all the classics can be staged: he is now offended, she feels letdown, she retaliates by disrespecting him, her stock goes up and she knows it, his stock goes down and he has no idea, and so on. However, if you collect yourself together and look out the office building window at the trees, streets and passers-by, if you call your family and then turn your gaze back to the current debate within the walls of the institution, then you immediately recognize in yourself and in others the constant threat of selling out every gesture of humanity to the operation.

So let's restate the question: What philosophy does someone need to buy into to be able to "love his servitude" (Jean-Jacques Rousseau) in this situation? After all, we do not want to think that we are doomed, we want to be well and we want to be successful. *Moral relativism* is the only theory that makes it possible to declare this manipulative culture morally unsuspicious. The relativist's slogans are: "Everyone has his own reality," or even more embarrassingly: "Perception is reality"; "You are right and I am right, each in his own way!" The argumentative obliteration of this feel-good theory for careerists is simple.

For if each had his own reality, we would *together* know nothing about reality. We could then only tell each other about our impressions, but this conversation could never yield agreement on common knowledge. And also the relativistic assertion that everybody has his own reality could then not be known *together*. If one assumes that relativism is true, then it becomes clear that it can only be just as true or false as any other statement one can think of. So there would be no reason to accept it and to reject deviant claims. Moral relativism is merely the illusion of a philosophy; one could also say: the abandonment of philosophy, of reasoning about what is good and the ways to achieve it, disguised as philosophy.

This surrender of critical reflection is seductively attractive. Because only if we can assure each other in a credible way that there are no moral truths and thus no fundamental human rights, i.e., no *real* demands on us - only then can unscrupulous careerists find it legitimate to manipulate their fellow human beings to the letter. Only if there is no truth, is every statement legitimate from one or another *perspective*: viewed from *some* point of view, anything goes.

No one is then responsible for the consequences of the actions taken by his institution, and presumably one also escapes personal responsibility. It seems to be quite unproblematic then, as an official, to be merely a 'cog in the wheel.' Reckless opportunism towards employees and unprincipled sycophancy towards superiors are then at least harmless - if not indeed 'smart,' 'clever,' 'skillful,' in terms of one's own career progress.

"Truth is surrendered to relativity and man to power" (Theodor W. Adorno). Once relativism has been accepted, the occurrence of professionalism and leadership as previously described becomes very sinister: Employees and superiors lie to each other in a well-regulated way and have in any case a professional justification to do so; wanting to call someone a liar only shows one's own unprofessionalism. Moral relativism enables the inmates of our 'worlds of work' to glorify the morally idiotic professionalism they owe to their company.

This point is very simple and therefore very difficult to *really* understand: The industrial system creates a demand in all of us for a fantasy of relief that lets us morally 'off the hook'. And where there is such cultural demand, there is supply. It is not absurd to think of cultural history as the emergence of such needs for explanation or justification, which then, while they are still emerging, bring forth the means of their satisfaction. In this sense, industrial society *causes* moral relativism, i.e., complete loss of moral reflection, and, in the end, numbness against the consequences of one's own thoughts and actions.

The athlete of this discipline of 'anything goes' is the ambitious person. He wants to make sure that the others see him just as they would have him. Ambition brings success and a pseudo-moral satisfaction - a recognized decency that I can earn and maintain through professionalism, without ever having to think about others or question myself. For success is assigned to those who are *unscrupulously* pragmatic in the sense of the institution's purpose.

However, our entire European cultural tradition is shaped by the ultimately correct and indispensable view that there are standards for our actions that are independent of our subjective interests and opinions. The indispensable role of a decisive authority in this respect has been played by different types of convictions through the ages: God's revelation, the categorical imperative, human rights, the integrity of the human person, etc. Only the acceptance of such standards makes it possible to create and develop a culture.

For what is culture other than an established value system, a living "connection between theory and practice" (according to Alasdair MacIntyre)? That is why the acceptance of norms that are absolutely binding for us is always present in the public consciousness of strongly developed cultures. (So much so that even state criminals always put a lot of work into selling their wars of aggression and mass murders as "humanitarian interventions" or "peacemaking". Obviously, this cultural factor is taken into account in the population to be defrauded, and this is mirrored faithfully in the propaganda strategy of warring parties.)

It is precisely because of this widespread awareness of ultimate moral obligations that moral relativism is so appealing. It soothes our consciences and gives the seal of philosophical legitimacy, the semblance of reasonableness and even wisdom to our opportunism and our narrowest, most unoriginal self-interest. Once, in fact, the day before Christmas vacation, I experienced the following exchange with colleagues from a leadership team; I opened it with a question: "Do you know what the biggest bullshit was that I heard this year? *Everyone has their own reality!*" The response of two men with decades of academic education and management experience was passionate and committed: "But - that's exactly how it is! That's what you have to understand, that's the most important thing in life!" Well, in their life, perhaps.

Industrial society's need for moral reassurance through relativism, combined with the convenience for the individual to swallow this pill, is an enormously powerful force of history. This connection explains the morally unscrupulous pragmatism of modern functionaries who have brought unprecedented suffering and destruction as well as material prosperity to the world. Moral relativism declares as irrelevant precisely those moral scruples that our industrial society imposes on us and that our professionalism is supposed to put out of our minds for the sake of operational efficiency.

In this way, doing what is good for our institution and what brings success for ourselves is declared to be the right morality. This unscrupulous pragmatism of professionalism, free of all fetters, is the dark secret of the mass crimes of the last centuries. It is also effective in the inhumane structures of human exploitation and environmental destruction, in which we, as their rulers and apparent profiteers, live comfortably, though hopefully not entirely at peace with ourselves.

8 Ambition and death

The cultural situation described up to this point induces and also trains us to extinguish our own moral life or never to develop one at all. Against this background, "ambition and death" is what I call the normal fate, the normal course of living and dying that industrial society has in store for us. The philosophical stance that allows me to grasp this common fate as the doom we must guard against is a simple humanism.

This is my core belief: Man's self-directed life is the meaning of the world - its whole meaning, all that is recognizable to me. And no matter what my fellow human beings believe, whether they are Christians or Muslims or atheists or Buddhists - we can agree on *this* meaning. After all, it makes sense for all of us: practicing Christianity or Islam is also a form of self-directed life, which the humanist considers to be of supreme value. And only in a society in which the practice of religion is protected can the Christian and the Muslim lead a life in accord with their own standards - just as I as a humanist can follow my beliefs here, which do not entail reliance on higher powers.

But in an open society, I can also renounce being myself; I can give up my life, and that is in my opinion the real "sin," the fundamental moral error for which we and our society then pay dearly. To become a dedicated functionary for the operation of society and the service of its rulers is a betrayal of the very shaping of my own life - a betrayal of myself. For whenever a person abandons his reflection - i.e., his reservation against everything that is supposedly self-evident - that is when his self-determination, his moral independence (autonomy) ends.

For a humanist, this feels as if the world would end *pars pro toto*. For if we are correct in our interpretation that in modern times only the will of man, set upon himself, can order the world and improve the fate of mankind, then the self-betrayal of the functionary is nothing less than the abdication of the world's government *en miniature*. Of course, government continues, except that I, as a functionary, play no part in determining its direction. I just go along with it, a pliable servant of whomever and whatever. We must not do that.

Telling the truth

At the beginning of the previous chapter, I claimed that our lives *must not* simply consist of a career in the world of work, and just now I have already issued another ban. Both statements are injunctions, both claim authority for clear and unambiguous insight. I say that I am right and that disregarding or misunderstanding the insights offered can even turn out to be morally disastrous. This is a behavior that moral relativism radically prohibits and which, from its point of view, is either an embarrassing mistake or an expression of arrogance. Someone claims to put forward more than just one opinion among many, indeed, he claims to be telling *the truth*!

That is correct, but not to be confused with delusions of infallibility. I simply take a definitive stand. The point of view I present and argue here is based on the best reasons that I have been able to give from my life experience and from the work of my mind; these reasons are, to the best of my ability, arranged into an overall picture that seems to me to reveal the reality of our present in essential respects. I present the reasons that make this point of view compelling for me - and therefore potentially for others, as well. This is my attempt to tell the truth. Direct revelation of God has eluded me until now; this is the best I can offer.

But the attempt to tell the truth, knowing full well that I will not be able to do so in the end - this attempt is necessary if you are not at peace with the world. "The truth must be told because of the conclusions it imposes on our behavior" (Bertholt Brecht). Only the attempt to find and speak the truth makes a new beginning possible, a fresh start in a better direction. For the reasons we give each other for our views are not merely subjective, they are at least intersubjective, i.e., they can be communicated to others.

We can make each other smarter and learn continuously if we dare to take a stand and actively defend it. Doing this while at the same time and for the sake of humble appearances speaking as if one did not consider one's convictions to be true, would be disingenuous. I may be mistaken in my theories - but not about the fact that I seek the truth. To conceal this rhetorically would be to curtsy before a relativist zeitgeist that does not dare to take a stand because it wishes to spare itself the responsibility for the scandalous state of our world.

If we try to tell each other the truth, we come into conflict. So be it. For if we succeed in telling the truth, then this just means that we have presented one another with matters of fact we cannot deny. And if we do not like these facts, then we (also undeniably) have a problem; from a philosophical point of view, hopefully this would be no less than a *fundamental* problem. It is precisely the raising of such an awareness that is the goal when we try to tell each other the truth. Even before hearing each other out, we intuitively resist entering such an awareness when we are uncomfortable with such new insights. Then a dispute ensues.

A person's philosophy, the craft that he imagines his life to be, is considerably the most fruitful starting point for a dispute - for the fundamental struggle that one must work through in order to become himself. Everything else is merely discussion, trivial banter without painful and joyful results that can be "incorporated" (einverleibt; Friedrich Nietzsche), and that will forever haunt us if, once achieved, we wished to set them aside, self-deceivingly.

Therefore it is neither an embarrassing mistake nor a matter of sheer arrogance in seeking to tell the truth. But such an error and fatal arrogance is to be found in relativism: the lack of a well-conceived standpoint is sold to fellow human beings as a general principle, as proper philosophy. Relativism is actually the abandonment of reason, the abdication of our independent judgement - the unconditional submission to the powers that happen to be most influential and that could therefore shape us into what we have already become.

So why *may* our life path not simply consist of a career in the world of work? In the previous chapters we have already answered individual parts of this question. Perhaps the remarks on conformism, existence as functionaries, and the deceptive, because humanly empty, "standard program" of rational work and success already were already sufficient; perhaps they have already given rise to a certain skepticism as to whether participating and abiding suffices for us. But there is still a crucial discussion required by this philosophy, a final commentary on this diagnosis of the present age. This discussion takes the concept of ambition as its point of departure.

Thinking in terms of honor and ambition, we can sharpen everything to a picture of the ordinary fate that industrial society holds in store for us. Ambition, the driving force behind most careers, is the driving force that weds us to this fatal course of life. We must escape it to avoid degenerating into mere functionaries; and if we absolutely must have a career, we should avoid having it out of ambition. Leading a life of our own, one that unfolds more or less along the lines of our autonomous design, and in which we recognize ourselves, *does not mean* living a happy or successful life. It means living a life that we, as *reasonable* beings, can account and take responsibility for. As beings who are capable of being and who therefore *want to be* masters of themselves.

We must not *only*, not *simply* have a career in the world of work, as our purpose in life, because we thereby abandon our moral independence, becoming accomplices to any and all injustice. The common fate of ambition has a moral and a political aspect - the failing moral person is the accomplice to social injustices. The two dimensions, the moral and the political, are inseparable.

Approaching ambition

The culture of our present tends to loosen the two staples that give our lives support and direction: the ideas of self and reality. In the fifth chapter we saw how industrial society offers us a standard identity based on rational work and the corresponding success, as a home, as a stable place in the world. We now take up these thoughts once more, but with a view to ambition. *Ambition* takes center stage here in our reflections; in my analysis and view, it represents *pseudo-moral madness*. A better understanding of this madness is the final and most important objective of this philosophy. For the *delusions* of its members express the operational needs of a society: They indicate the exact way in which we must become insane in order to participate.

The *moral* insanity of ambition (that can have a surface appearance of moral behavior) is the basic attitude that our world of work cultivates in us. Pursuit of the pseudo-morality of ambition and success is a form of insanity because it represents my own voluntary self-transformation into a functionary, my moral self-abandonment. Tragically and ironically, the industrial system ensures that during this progressive self-abandonment, an appearance of distinguishing myself as a human being, of developing my character, can arise.

This pathology is at the center of our present-day culture. Ambition is the social operating system of our institutions because self-uncertainty is the predominant result of growing up in the order of prestige; we have all been trained to become scouts and managers of foreign expectations. Ambition is therefore also the *piety* of industrial society. It embodies the striving to placate through our visible submission the power that can grant us salvation from our misery.

Only those who understand this madness can consider in detail their own life, from one situation to another, as to what it might take for them *not* to go mad. The result of this philosophy, its actual teaching about empty success (*Erfolgsleere*, in the German title), is not a fixed set of recommendations on how to arrange our lives. It has to do for me with forming an awareness of the force of ambition; to recognize its power over us in order to be able to escape it, at least now and again. If these insights seem too negative and too 'elitist,' just try multiplying them by -1 for your situation in life, as you learned in school, and ask: If this is the threat my ambition presently poses to me, what is the way to protect myself against it right now?

Like any concept of moral weight, the term 'ambition' occupies a familiar but not necessarily clearly defined space in our language. First of all, we must note that honorable conduct is not necessarily an expression of ambition and does not necessarily presuppose it. It is oftentimes with an action or a person precisely the clear absence of motives commonly considered "ambitious," such as the desire for advancement, greed for money, etc., that makes us call them honorable or decent.

Where honor is spoken of, where there is praise and criticism, where status is granted and denied, ambition need not necessarily be involved. That is why ambition is a phenomenon that requires separate discussion and analysis. It cannot be understood simply on the basis of the previous chapters and our customary use of language around honor and status.

The German term *Ehrgeiz* comes from Middle High German, where the adjective "ergetic" was used in the 16th century as a composition of "honor" and "stingy" (in the sense of greedy or avaricious). We spoke earlier at length about our constant work in navigating social networks, in which we achieve and maintain our status in the order of prestige and make this possible for others, as well. The historical root of the term fits this picture because in this modern social fabric, the ambitious person is the one who is envious, as it were, greedily anxious to control his external image.

When forming a series of sentences with the word 'ambition' and saying it before oneself, one notices that, according to current usage, ambition can seemingly be something good or bad - depending entirely on that to which the ambition is directed. This view can already be found in general encyclopedias published around the turn of the 20th century. It also shows that success and achievement seem to be closely linked to ambition, as well as a fear of failure and defeat.

At the end of this philosophy, we have to work our way out of these vagueries, which are all neither altogether true nor completely false. Recognition of the central pathology of our zeitgeist depends on the notions of honor (in the sense of prestige or status) and ambition being freed from the systemic folklore that is attached to them. Honor and ambition must be analyzed and interpreted together - for they are closely interrelated in our history as well as in the matter itself.

The emptiness of honor

In the chapter on the order of prestige, we saw how the coordinating discipline of a mutual ritualism of respect creates order in times of ideological disagreement. The game of honor, of paying respect, is the moral reality of modern times; our "constitutional ritual" is the honoring of others. We can take it as a constant tribute of our thinking and doing to the presumed will of the others.

This expresses the principle of modern statehood, according to which my will is *in principle* as much the sovereign of the world as that of any other person, because it is our human will, not a divine will, that underlies the texts of our constitutions. In our everyday lives, we administer, shape, propagate, and also bear our personal honor, for better and for worse. At the same time, we encourage and criticize others, whose status we confirm through our showing of attention. In this way, we make our social existence largely predictable for each other.

This balancing act of so many individuals with one another and in ever-changing ensembles of actors revolves, however, around an *empty* object. The golden calf around which we dance is a cardboard dummy. This has already been alluded to in the chapters on the order of prestige and on the apparent salvation that success and rational work promise us. We spoke there, for example, of the inner instability of people whose being was structured by becoming a functionary, whose pragmatism knows no bounds and who can in principle be mobilized for any purpose.

At the bottom of the emptiness of a zealous functionary's self lies the moral emptiness of external honor - of prestige, credit, and status in the eyes of others. The tragedy of the zealous functionary is that he tries to make himself a particular someone, a personality, by (over) fulfilling other people's expectations; in reality, however, he becomes more and more a nobody: a "man without qualities" (Robert Musil), but with a sophisticated instinct for obedience.

The vapidity of honor and status can be understood with a detour via a subject that, admittedly, will appear farfetched. Let's talk for a moment about *the weather*. The movements of winds and clouds, the buildup and discharge of humidity, the interplay of high and low pressure areas, etc. - that is the weather, the actual state of our atmosphere. This actual state determines how the harvest will turn out, it signifies whether certain dynamic factors will play out as a mild breeze or a hurricane. The weather forecast, on the other hand, is not the weather itself: it is our discussion of the weather as we understand it and our prediction of its development.

A person's honor (or social status) and his actual moral quality relate to each other in much the same way as do the weather report and the actual weather. The talk of honor reflects, sometimes clearly and sometimes approximately, the moral and legal rules *actually* accepted in a society. The status that a society grants a person depends solely upon these rules and says nothing about the actual moral quality of that person.

The concept of honor anchored in a shared language reflects the accepted standard of a society; it is its moral weather forecast. It only tells us how society *actually* imagines good and evil, right and wrong, and what its members *usually* praise or blame each other for. In this analogy, the *actual* moral quality of what happens in a society corresponds to the *actual* weather.

What is *actually* happening here - quite independently of what our established and accustomed code of honor would call it? For example, isn't what our established concept of honor would consider personal achievement and merit, primarily the predictable effect of the undeserved privileging of individuals based on material inequality? Or is professionalism not *actually*, as we have argued before, merely structured thoughtlessness to preserve the industrial system?

This "actually," i.e., the "wait a minute!" that the person who pronounces these words asserting, can only be truly upheld and defended if the speaker refers to his value concepts. For these give him the yardstick by which he asserts an objection to the actual thinking and doing, that is, to the current concept of honor in his society. It is his moral concepts that give him the strength for this moral intervention, the strength by virtue of which he expresses his will that things should be different than what they are.

Let us briefly circle and better familiarize ourselves with this fundamental difference between honor and morality - because growing up in the order of honor makes us unlearn this distinction and we therefore have to acquire it anew. To speak of honor or shame in our society means to take a survey of our surroundings and say what we *are used to* evaluating in this or that way. It means giving the moral weather report.

The conferment or denial of honor, praise or blame is the *invocation of* existing moral or legal norms. By these means, we can discipline others and ourselves, at least to the extent that we fear these rules and norms. But the confirmation or diminution of reputation and status is *not itself* an expression of one's own value concepts, just as the weather report is *not itself* the weather.

If one expresses praise or a rebuke, one can only make it comprehensible by immediately referring to this or that concrete value system that is accepted in society, be it moral or legal. Only this reference makes it clear what is meant when the person concerned is criticized or praised. Taken by itself, on its own, speaking of honor or disgrace is not *normatively* significant; reference to an established norm always requires that substance be given to such claims. The concept of honor itself is empty.

In the customary routines of praise and rebuke, in the status struggle within a society, one can get the wrong impression of what it means to conduct a moral discussion - i.e., to explain *one's own* values, have them examined and criticized, and react to this criticism from one's own value standpoint. That points to a confusion. It is morally and legally meaningless in itself to describe someone as a human being or some of his actions as honorable or shameful, to praise or rebuke them. Because this only means that the established, accepted values of society approve or disapprove of his behavior. This does not mean that we have entered into the discussion decisive for our life, about which values are the right ones.

To again take up a manner of speaking we addressed earlier: discussions of honor operate within the realm of the *simple thinking and doing* in a given society, with which it maintains its established standards and power structures. These discussions do *not* operate within the realm of *reflection and action*, in which individuals and societies consciously define their own value standards and then measure their actions against this yardstick. The whole discussion about honor is *rational* in the sense of established values and norms, but it is not yet *reasonable* in the sense that the question of the *right* values is expressly posed asked and answered.

The confusing of these levels of our practical life is consequential; it is the cultural heart of the darkness of stale routine, outrageous indifference and efficiency that our industrialized civilization has brought into the world (beside enormous material wealth, inequality, and environmental destruction). For whoever thinks that they can already act morally by simply carrying out the learned instructions of their society and amassing thereby as many advantages for themselves as possible, does not know the difference between rational doing and reasonable action, between success and moral value.

A person like that can be counted on: He will always participate in what is being transacted, because he does not know anything else and does not understand the process of discovering alternatives through reflection and autonomous action. For anyone who wants to make something better out of himself and, as a citizen, out of his society, the confusion between honor and morality is disastrous. "For those of us who care," for those of us who are not oblivious to everything, as Chris Hedges likes to say in his speeches against American oligarchy.

Ambition is pseudo-moral madness

Industrial society casts its hook into the life of our soul. It subordinates people who are centered on reputation and status, on external honor, and who therefore *look beyond and around themselves* through the eyes of restless ambition. Our ambition is the harness thrown over our shoulders and within whose (more or less) padded straps we then pull the cart of industrial society. The athletes and ascetics of this conformation, who place themselves under the yoke with zeal and determination, are the ambitious ones. Ambition is the guiding principle of industrial society and also - as we shall see - its characteristic form of madness.

The constant recommendation of ambition and our schooling in its logic have in their favor systematic and at the same time very practical reasons. The world of work needs functionaries as employees and superiors for its operation and continuity. The ambitious person is optimally suited both roles - because he depends more than anyone else on redemption through institutionally organized success and is therefore compliant, eager and diligent. On closer inspection, the world of work turns out to be the realm of ambition and the ambitious.

So what exactly is ambition? Ambition is the planned and eager struggle to adapt to external expectations, i.e., to what others (supposedly or probably or actually) want from me, before they are willing to grant me the success they have to grant. Ambition is the planned optimization of the image others have of my person - to be sure, not their image of me in terms of *my own* value concepts, but in terms of the value concepts *I* insinuate to *them*. In other words: The ambitious person wants to appear (and perhaps even *be*) as others would like him to be.

The good Christian is interested in loving his neighbor in a charitable way. The *ambitious* Christian is concerned that all others may *notice* how much and how charitably he loves his neighbor. For this reason, he diligently presents his love within his parish in a way that he considers to be applaudable; in the company, he will then want to make sure, according to the same pattern, to impress upon his boss how much he, in particular, loves him. The content is subordinated to the outer form and, depending on the strength of ambitious motives, subordinated in every all-important detail of practical life.

'Ambition' is the name for a battle that can never be won, viz. to fulfill *in the opinion* of others the demands that they make upon me. The concern of the ambitious for his status is a self-occupation with others, it is ultimately a sad affair. For this concern is directed at others, it wants to penetrate their thinking and feeling, and in this sense it is humanly oriented and interested in other people; only not *authentically*.

A person-to-person connection is established, but *not* in order to really come and align themselves together or support each other in the pursuit of shared values. The connection is made by the ambitious person with a fundamentally manipulative intention. He wants something from the others, he wants their confirmation and approval, as well as the material trophies of success; he wants to see his ambition satisfied and, in a sense, draws on the presence of the others to quench his thirst.

But this very satisfaction is impossible for several reasons. First, ambition is distracting and in practice it often amounts to self-sabotage. The ambitious are in a state of consciousness that never allows them to simply be where they are and do what they intend to do. Rather, the ambitious are always at the same time standing beside themselves, assessing the quality of their current position and conduct by the standard they presume is being applied to them by others. The mental eye of the ambitious person always wants to be the eye of the other person, wants to assume the other person's perspective in order to maneuver accordingly and calculate the effects of one's own moves.

Not only does handling one's attention in such a two-pronged way reduce the objective chances of succeeding at anything one might undertake; it is also exhausting. An incessant 'status calculation' must be artificially added to the usual perception of our environment.

Montesquieu aptly points this out with a simple observation: "The slightest object that affects our senses is capable of taking away our consuming thoughts of ambition."

Yet another, purely external circumstance thwarts the intentions of the ambitious. In mass society, at literally every moment other people are "the others" from whom the ambitious person seeks to draw the nourishment for his soul. The status gain that the Porsche driver strives for with his neighbor is already completely lost the moment he has to park in the neighboring street one evening - because nobody knows him there and his demonstration of status loses its audience. You don't see neighbor Manfred, the successful doctor and investor, getting out of his brandname advertising machine, but you simply see a man in his mid-fifties pretending to be 35. Even the ultimate goal of many ambitious people, celebrity or general fame, is actually only "the advantage of being known to those who don't know you" (Nicolas Chamfort). In the struggle for status, you always start with your stone, like Sisyphus, at the very bottom of the hill, with each new encountered situation.

This also explains the emaciated physique of the most ambitious people, and their addictions, with which they build an imaginary compensation into their everyday life at the expense of their health. All in all, the "diseases of affluence" that we contract within this order are actually "diseases of poverty" – poverty of meaning. For what really remains when we subtract overabundant food, hypnotic entertainment orgies ("binge-watching") and rigidly emptied days of rest ("holidays")?

We cannot moderate ourselves in the pleasures of eating, drinking, smoking, entertainment and sexuality. First we control ourselves in order to professionally carry out meaningless work and to maintain our status, accordingly. Then we are consciously unrestrained in our enjoyment - perhaps because we somehow feel that we deserve a "reward" for this laborious continuous production of an illusion; perhaps, as well, because we no longer really *know* anything apart from our conformism in the acquisition of money for the sake of which it was worth restraining ourselves; perhaps for all these reasons.

Ambition therefore involves selling out to others my own value judgement of things. Instead of judging myself, I ask myself how others will judge things, and I then act on that estimation. That means, in every ambitious moment taken by itself, the surrender of my own judgement. But in this way, one's own life, which consists in working on oneself in the light of experience, is short-circuited.

The tool of this craft, of our life, is our reflection, in which we not only want to recognize what is generally accepted, but with the help of which we want to decide for ourselves what is worth fighting for. Ambition is not the "death of thought," as Ludwig Wittgenstein says, but the death of *reflection* and therefore the end of man as a moral person. This is the betrayal of one's own self that was mentioned at the beginning of this chapter.

For man cannot be himself without his own reflection, i.e., cannot exist as a moral person. Without reasonable reflection he exists only as a subject of prevailing conditions, a functionary of the world as it happens to be. Therefore, ambition is the logical opposite of morality, its counterpower. For morality consists precisely in exercising an objection to ordinary thought and action on the basis of one's own value judgments, where that is deemed necessary.

Where rational work and the ambitious pursuit of success feel like the right, morally justifiable or even praiseworthy life, and no deficit is felt, we are therefore faced with *pseudo-moral insanity*. We consider an eagerly pursued career to be our life and have morally ceased to exist. This madness is ambition.

There is also a social, a political consequence to this. Ambitious people are inwardly *turned towards* the prestige and the power of society and its representatives. They fantasize about holding high offices and crave fame and recognition. They are therefore *turned away* from their own value concepts (if they have developed any at all). Therefore, the ambitious person is subject to a unique powerlessness; not only is he morally incapable of changing himself, he is also politically impotent.

For the ambitious person cannot endanger the functioning of the current society by acting outside of the established rules and theories, he cannot change his society. This is the astonishing paradox of ambition: the ambitious person loses his power over himself and over the social circumstances of life *precisely by turning to them* so resolutely and thereby turning away from himself. For example, the German Greens started out with a peace policy and the demand to leave NATO; then the ambition of the functionaries overtook the party and the former blockaders of military bases became advocates of the illegal war in Yugoslavia.

The moral impotence of ambitious man arises from his eagerness to strictly adhere to the socially prescribed ways of thinking and acting. The socially disciplinary effect of ambition is immense: for ambition is an expression of the surrender of moral reflection. Thus, insofar as someone is ambitious, he is not present as a moral person, but as a subject of the prevailing conditions and those who are ruling. The ambitious person is incapable of shaping his life and his societal circumstances, but rather optimally suited to their operation. He is a functionary. The pseudo-moral insanity of ambition is the operating system of a society of functionaries.

The usual fate

To cultivate the supposed virtue of ambition in oneself is therefore to purchase the entre-billet to our institutions and to begin our "ascent" along the different career paths that are intended to fully occupy us. The ambitious man is the zealot of conformism, the willing executor of the ruling principle, and therefore the morally defunct ruler of the world - the world as it is and as it must remain, with him as its leader frozen in formulas and phrases.

Ambition is the path to inner emptiness, the fundamental sabotage of the growth and development of a stable, value-oriented and therefore resilient self. It is the program to completely do away with people who want to better themselves and their society and who could therefore endanger the status quo. The apparent fulfillment that ambition can grant is only empty success (*Erfolgsleere*). Inner emptiness in success tells the whole truth about industrial society.

But the normal program of ambition, our usual fate, means good business. Because of its truly dehumanizing principle, industrial society needs and promotes a special kind of conformism, a pseudo-individualization that promises to fill this existential void: an increasingly delicate consumerism. Products and services are produced industrially with a view to previously identified types of consumers. The consumer with highly differentiated needs is therefore a perverse construct. He is presented and understood as a type of the highest individuality and originality; in fact, the emotional state in which he fancies he has to buy this or that is the dead expression of skillful manipulation.

Herbert Marcuse saw this and summarized the problem, admittedly in pointed and dramatic fashion: "Free choice from a wide variety of goods and services does not mean freedom if these goods (...) maintain social control over a life of toil and fear." The consumer's mind and emotions are imbued with statistically determined standard desires, and these he pursues. Through industrious conformism, conscious, picky consumption simulates individuality where morally there is none - ironically, and to the scorn of the eager consumer. This presents a superficial relief from the modern trauma of forlornness that ambition brings us. The provision of this relief is required by the system; the alliance of industrial ambition and boundless consumerism is an elective affinity.

The desires that the good consumer is meant to chase after are summarized by the concept of a 'brand,' which is astonishing in many respects. The brand is that which in a product is *not* the thing or the service itself. It is the assumption by others about the thing or service that is meticulously constructed and controlled by the producer, and so 'branding' is from the outset a largely nonsensical and essentially deceptive undertaking. From a social point of view, it is nonsensical because the duplication of products and services with the same utility, which makes branding necessary in the first place, is economically wasteful.

To those who defend this practice in the name of competition, which (we are told) is the only source of progress and development, there is only one brief reply to be made: Psychologists have long known that nothing causes more stress and makes people unhappier than competition. Innovation comes about when people are allowed to discourse reasonably and freely with each other and act together in solidarity - *not* when they are pitted against each other in a battle to outdo each other by the standard of the prejudices and predilections of their superiors.

I also said that marketing in the individual cases of certain products and services is a fraudulent venture. After all, if its features provide compelling reasons for buying a given product or service, 'branding' it would not be necessary - accurate information would be sufficient to attract buyers. Branding is required only when a product is *not* reasonably distinguishable from other products or services of the same kind because the utility sought is equally provided by all of them.

This is why in TV commercials we see "cars taking off into space" (Noam Chomsky) instead of simply being informed about their characteristics. The brand is that specious characteristic of my new three-day beard wash gel, which draws long-haired, full-bosomed photo models to my cheeks (or, in the case of the new eyelash volume brush with gold dust infusion, daring, cool-looking super sportsmen with super sports cars to my chest, according to gender). Marketing produces occult non-features of the product, which are fraudulently presented to the potential buyer as actual qualities. By its very nature, advertising is objectively unfounded distinction. Therefore, advertising stops of its own accord when a product or service is unrivaled. There is no advertisement by the public water utility companies in Germany. There is no need for advertising if nobody has to be cheated.

The special trick of marketing, its psychological consummation, is that people pay massive surcharges for a sign on a shirt or for lettering on a watch, in contrast to equally useful products - only to then strut around the world as advertising media for these nonsensical products. The well-trained consumer cues for the opportunity to pay an exaggerated price for things in order to show off his status in this way. The mannequins of industry dress at their own expense, fancying themselves to be individualists, and are often even treated as such.

In the same way, the "personal brand," whose construction is preached to us by the conformist clergy in the career pages of major newspapers and by bad coaches, is the individual's consciously controlled assumption of others about himself. This brand, just like the "style" of the consumer individualist bought up and stitched together through shopping for mass products, is also an individuality without life, like the whole existence of a merely ambitious person. Marketing is the social version of the very erosion practice that ambition represents in the life of the individual.

Industrial society, the realm of ambition, is the space of a morally unscrupulous pragmatism of functionaries. Superiors define the professionalism of their field without reference to reality, only with view to the 'world of work' found in their institution. The functionaries execute this professionalism. Their ambition drives both sides forward and keeps them from reflecting.

Supervisors and employees, two types of functionaries, mutually conceal their moral sellout to the institution, guided by the perverse cult of professionalized humanity, their pseudo-morality of success and their pseudo-reason of rationality. Those who have enough thoughtfulness to look for an excuse hum the comforting song of relativism, whose refrain is: "Everyone has his own reality! No one is right! But everyone has a perspective!" The result of this dance of death was the moral bankruptcy of our order in the mass crimes of the last centuries, and may spell the ecological ruin of our planet in the next step.

The empty self of many inhabitants of industrial society, standardized on rational work and the striving for success, and spun into the routines of consumption, cannot contradict the established patterns of thought and action. It is neutral to everything, allows everything to happen, stops nothing and promotes nothing but the usual. The emptiness of ambitious work, its moral nothingness, is the decisive reason for the habitual course of things everywhere. So if we have something to criticize in the usual course of things, in ourselves and in our society, we must discard ambition. Everything begins with reflection, with the desire to know what is actually going on with us. Then we can ask what should be, and begin our life.

There is no place for arrogance in this striving. The professional functionaries, among whose ranks we ourselves are and with whom we deal at work, are to be considered as *whole moral persons* just like ourselves - because we cannot see into anyone and therefore owe everyone this basic respect in the first place. Even the polemically trenchant passages of this book do not intend to claim that the structures in which someone is stuck would determine him hopelessly, perhaps even *force* him into taking on a pathological character.

Such an assertion would be arrogance in the negative sense, and it would contradict this philosophy. After all, we have just argued and continually emphasized that through our reflection we are always beyond the conditions in which we exist - that, in principle, we can always change ourselves and our conditions. Why else would I have written this book, and why else would you want to read it?

At the same time, however, after the thought process unfolded in these eight chapters, it is clear that we can hardly develop unhindered as moral persons in the world of work. The structures work against this. Where we exhaust ourselves and others in rational work and competition for success, there is no humanity. It can only be found where we meet in compassion and reasonable exchange and try together to achieve betterment for ourselves and our society. For these are the real human activities, not merely functional ones; they alone are actually directed towards reality, being as they are not merely pragmatic in the sense of anonymous, particular purposes.

We must therefore look for and create spaces in our lives in which this actual human interaction is at the center. What these living spaces can look like depends on the individual. There are therefore no generally applicable teachings in the philosophical tradition about what we should do with our lives. Neither does philosophy provide us with the one, indisputable picture of the just society that we would have to build together. But there are valuable indications throughout the philosophical tradition of how we can succeed in cultivating our own living space against the resistance and pressure of conformism in society. I have spoken of an approach to this, as well as I understand it, in the chapters on "Philosophizing as the Craft of Life" and on "Morality and Conformity."

You may conclude: "Oh, Andrick recommends a little inner reflection and political engagement after work!" There is nothing wrong with this conclusion; as Kant says: "The world will not go under because fewer evil people wander it." However, Andrick recommends a more far-reaching insight. Only fellowship with others who share the same value judgments opens up a space of fulfilling activity that appeals to us as whole human beings and makes us come alive.

Experiences of such a common striving can certainly be found in our various institutions, be those administrations, parties, or companies - when we are in the right place and can work on something that we feel is meaningful and helpful for everyone. But this joyful community with others remains unstable and is under constant threat by the distorting influences of industrial operations, which this book is about. Gainful employment alone is in most cases a fluctuating, ultimately too narrow a basis for a life worth living.

This is the deeper wisdom behind the voluntary *engagement* toward goals that go beyond our own destiny and that we can therefore share in solidarity with others. And the life experience that carries this insight will also drive a corresponding commitment in the long term. Because the individual success around which the general competitive race revolves, is something we can only have when many, many others do *not* enjoy it. This is how this race separates us from others, and that is why a successful career as such is not a fulfilling path in life. As human beings, we find fulfillment only when we take an interest in others and seek with them to realize the best for our community. For this reason, an enlightened life leads to public action, to politics.

A personal way out

This last section will be short. For a person who wants to lead his life according to his own value concepts does not need any schematic instructions about what to do. His life consists precisely in the effort to find this out for himself and to act according to his insights. To offer "recipes" here could only end in self-righteous preaching. In the end, respect for diversity and individuality, not 'philosophical instruction' is required. Every path out of empty success is an individual, a personal path.

I would therefore like to conclude with a careful consideration that borders on shame and that, precisely for this reason, might possibly serve as a starting point for the reader's further reflection. In the end, as in life in general, it must be about *love*. This may sound surprising at the end of a book about morality, society, institutions, ambition and more. We usually only speak of love in religion and in relationships; exclusively in situations that we regard as private, highly personal and intimate.

Moreover, the word 'love' has become stale and the experience behind it unclear, because for a long time now everything that people have wanted to sell us has been draped in such a way that it is supposed to mobilize a little of the power and meaning of love and turn it into revenue. Anyone who speaks to us of "love" and "passion" beyond intimate relationships, often does so on the occasion of the market launch of the latest lipstick or sports car.

As a consequence, the decisive thing about love can first fall from sight and then from consciousness: that it belongs to the life of our soul to love - just as it belongs to our soul to be afraid of some things and to wonder about others. In this sense, love is not only the ecstatic exception of our life - like the infatuation of two people or the embrace of our children. Love is the decisive force of our inner life and our relationship to the world.

I can't explain what love is, but I know it anyway - we know it. Love can be observed. We love what we fight for, what we stand up for. Love shows in the unconditional loyalty and devotion to our partner and to our own children; but it also shows in the values that we wish to realize with all our might. We *do not* necessarily love what we are 'ready' or 'determined to fight for'; such claims could be mere life lies or a politician's phrases, from which, when push comes to shove, nothing at all may follow except the arid hint that one "now has responsibility for a family" or that "the situation is just different now."

We only really love what we are *really* fighting for - that for which we take risks and for which we compromise our immediate well-being, for whose sake we dare to take steps toward and into the unknown and the feared, and to accept suffering. This view of love means a lot to me, and it also means a lot to this philosophy. In my opinion, only our struggle for the beloved reveals who we really are. Socrates drank the cup of poison handed to him by the Athenians, because he was indeed a 'lover of wisdom,' a philosopher in the ancient Greek sense: he could have continued living only at the price of fundamental disagreement with his own insight, so he accepted death.

My parents love freedom because they fought for it when in 1971 they got into a rubber dinghy with my sister and some friends to escape the GDR dictatorship over the Baltic Sea. They loved freedom for the sake of their own dignity, but they also loved and still love it for the sake of their children's dignified lives. That is why they risked everything and put their lives on the line to gain freedom. This is how I know who they *really* are, aside from the routines of their work, the vicissitudes of family life and the suffering of old age.

Not everyone loves wisdom or freedom, because not everyone fights for it. This leads to another thought, which is at once the last and the first of this philosophy. Spinoza grasped it as a young man when he noted - perhaps astonished and frightened by the bottomless depth of his reflection - that our concepts of things cannot be called true or false, "just as love cannot be called true or false, but only good or bad." What is good love, what is bad love? If we can recognize a person's love by what that person is *actually* fighting for, then we can also formulate this question differently: What is worth fighting for, and what isn't?

We explained why so many in modern industrial society fight for the smoothest possible integration into a "world of work": because they love the reassuring regularity of a conformist existence; we analyzed why so many fight ambitiously for their careers (which they love); we thought about why some fight for the view that nobody is ever really right, but always just a proponent of one or another among many equally valid opinions: because they love the fake moral peace of mind that only relativism can provide; finally, we asked why so many give a good part of their lives and their means to endlessly increase and refine their consumption: because they love to cover up the experience of emptiness and show others their success so that their admiration may sustain them.

So let us ask ourselves what we are *actually* fighting for in our lives, and let us be honest about it. Then we can see who we are at present, and we can ask ourselves if we are already who we want to be for ourselves and others. This is the crucial question: Is my love good or bad? My answer puts me at the starting point of my life.